500 RECIPES FOR JAMS, PICKLES, CHUTNEYS

and preserves, fruit cheeses, jellies, marmalades,
conserves, fruit curds, ketchups, fruit sauces and syrups,
flavoured vinegars, bottling, home freezing

by Marguerite Patten

HAMLYN
LONDON · NEW YORK · SYDNEY · TORONTO

Contents

Cover photograph by Paul Williams

Published by The Hamlyn Publishing Group Limited
London · New York · Sydney · Toronto
Astronaut House, Feltham, Middlesex, England

First published 1963
Revised edition 1971
Fourteenth impression 1983

ISBN 0 600 35209 9

Printed and bound in Great Britain by R. J. Acford

Introduction

This is a book to help you enjoy the fruits of summer throughout the year.
Many people say that home-preserving is a dying art, but this is not entirely true, for in the country you will still find a great tradition of preserving of every kind. The only reason that prevents town housewives from doing the same is that they are more rushed and busy, and the ingredients are usually more expensive.

But if you buy fruits and vegetables in season, when they are at their best and cheapest, or better still use your own garden produce, you will be delighted at the money you will save.
Bottling, pickling, jam making, and deep-freezing are all simple processes, and give a tremendous feeling of satisfaction and achievement when you have finished.

Some Useful Facts and Figures

Notes on metrication

In case you wish to convert quantities into metric measures, the following tables give a comparison.

Solid measures

Ounces	Approx. grams to nearest whole figure	Recommended conversion to nearest unit of 25
1	28	25
2	57	50
3	85	75
4	113	100
5	142	150
6	170	175
7	198	200
8	227	225
9	255	250
10	283	275
11	312	300
12	340	350
13	368	375
14	396	400
15	425	425
16 (1 lb)	454	450
17	482	475
18	510	500
19	539	550
20 (1¼ lb)	567	575

Liquid measures

Imperial	Approx. millilitres to nearest whole figure	Recommended millilitres
¼ pint	142	150
½ pint	283	300
¾ pint	425	450
1 pint	567	600
1½ pints	851	900
1¾ pints	992	1000 (1 litre)

Note: When converting quantities over 20 oz first add the appropriate figures in the centre column, then adjust to the nearest unit of 25. As a general guide, 1 kg (1000 g) equals 2·2 lb or about 2 lb 3 oz. This method of conversion gives good results in nearly all cases, although in certain pastry and cake recipes a more accurate conversion is necessary to produce a balanced recipe.

Notes for American and Australian users

In America the 8-oz measuring cup is used. In Australia metric measures are now used in conjunction with the standard 250-ml measuring cup. The Imperial pint, used in Britain and Australia, is 20 fl oz, while the American pint is 16 fl oz. It is important to remember that the Australian tablespoon differs from both the British and American tablespoons. The British standard tablespoon, which has been used throughout this book, holds 17·7 ml, the American 14·2 ml, and the Australian 20 ml. A teaspoon holds approximately 5 ml in all three countries.

Oven Temperatures

The following chart gives conversions from degrees Fahrenheit to degrees Celsius (formerly known as Centigrade) recommended by the manufacturers of Electric Cookers.

Note: This table is an approximate guide only. Different makes of cooker vary and if you are in any doubt about the setting it is as well to refer to the manufacturer's temperature chart.

	°C	°F	Gas Mark
VERY COOL	110	225	$\frac{1}{4}$
	120	250	$\frac{1}{2}$
COOL	140	275	1
	150	300	2
MODERATE	160	325	3
	180	350	4
MODERATELY HOT	190	375	5
	200	400	6
HOT	220	425	7
	230	450	8
VERY HOT	240	475	9

All about jam making

Utensils for making jam

The right utensils are a help in producing good jam with the minimum of bother. Obviously if you only make small quantities of jam some of them would be unnecessary, but these are the things you should have:

Preserving pan – this is described on page 5 but a good big saucepan could take its place. Whatever utensil is used remember that copper or brass can spoil the colour of red fruits but help to keep green fruits green. Zinc or iron pans spoil both colour and flavour. Aluminium or copper pans do not spoil the colour or flavour, but one tends to lose any vitamin in fruits containing a high percentage of vitamin C.

Wooden spoon – choose a long handled spoon, so that you can stir without fear of the hot jam splashing on to your hand.

Jars – ordinary jam jars are not obtainable in shops so you must retain them from year to year. You can use bottling jars, etc.

Metal jug or heatproof glass jug – this is the easiest way of filling the pots. Have one with a handle so you can scoop up the jam without burning your fingers.

Perforated metal spoon – this is the best way of skimming the jam.

Large funnel – not essential, but if you fill the pots through this you keep them very clean.

Sugar thermometer – for testing the temperature of jams etc. See page 7.

Muslin – for tying peel, pips etc., in certain jams.

Covers – use proper jam pot covers to make certain the jam keeps well.

Labels – the stick-on-labels should be put on the jars when quite cold.

Preliminary preparation of fruit for jam making

The way in which you prepare the fruit will make a lot of difference to your finished jam.

1 Look over the fruit carefully – discard any bruised or damaged portions. With large fruit you need only cut away the spoilt part – with soft fruit discard the whole fruit.

2 Unless you have picked the fruit from your own garden after a spell of very fine weather, so you are certain that the fruit is very clean, it is wise to wash it. The best way to do this is to lay the fruit on fine sieves and gently pour water over it. If you actually immerse the fruit in water, it absorbs too much and will, in consequence, make your jam watery.

    (a) With soft fruits, transfer to absorbent kitchen paper to dry.

    (b) With firm hard fruits, dry with a cloth.

Try to avoid washing those fruits that are deficient in pectin, i.e. strawberries in particular, since the extra amount of water is not required. Strawberries however grow near the ground and are sometimes extremely dirty. Never wash in hot water as this softens the fruit too early.

3 In some recipes one will need to 'top and tail' the fruit, i.e. in the case of gooseberries. The easiest way to cut off the stalk and flower end (which is what is meant by the term 'top and tail') is to use a pair of sharp kitchen scissors. Ideally, one should 'top and tail' blackcurrants, but if you are prepared to soften the fruit well, this is not essential, although it obviously gives a less perfect jam. In jellies where the fruit is being put through a jelly bag, do not bother to do this.

4 To remove stones from hard fruit, cut with a stainless knife and take out the stones. If the fruit is slightly under-ripe you may find this difficult in which case leave the stones in and take them out after the fruit has softened.

To stone cherries, insert a fine new hairpin into the fruit with the bent end going into the cherry. Move this around until you feel it lock around the stone, then pull sharply and you will find it brings the stone with it. Do this over the preserving pan as you tend to bring juice out with the stone. Or use a cherry stoner.

If you are following a recipe where it says 1 lb. stoned fruit and you have left the stones in, allow an extra 2–4 oz. fruit.

5 When peeling fruit, use a stainless knife and peel as thinly as possible to waste the minimum of fruit.

If you wish to skin fruits, such as peaches, immerse for a few seconds in boiling water to loosen the skin, lift out, place in cold water to cool the fruit rapidly, and then skin.

Note

These preparations should be done just before making the jam as the moment you wash, stone or peel the fruit it is inclined to deteriorate.

Setting quality of fruits

Some fruits set more easily than others – due to the amount of pectin and acid they contain. It may seem that some recipes are a little out of proportion, but this is not the case. The amount of water and sugar has been carefully calculated so that you will get a jam that sets in the minimum of time. With fruits, that are lacking in setting quality, such as ripe cherries and strawberries, it is essential to use rather more fruit than sugar, with the addition of extra pectin and acid in the form of lemon juice or redcurrant juice.

Your preserving pan in jam making

This should be of sufficient size so the jam can boil rapidly without fear of it boiling over. A wide pan allows for rapid evaporation of the liquid, so reaching setting point more quickly. Use copper or aluminium but never use chipped enamel pans in jam making. A proper preserving pan has a handle from which the pan can be suspended when not in use which ensures that it has a good air circulation to keep it fresh. If you shut pans away in tightly closed cupboards and do not use them for some months, they often have a rather musty smell which can affect the taste of your jam.

Sugar to use in jam making
Special preserving sugar is the best, but you can use loaf or granulated sugar.

Brown sugar does not give such a good set to the jam. It does, however, produce a very delicious flavour, so you may like to try using 25% brown sugar and the rest white.

Honey in jam making – honey gives a splendid flavour to jam, but it does not allow the jam to set firmly. You can, however, use 25% honey and 75% sugar for a firm set, or 50% honey and 50% sugar for a softer jam.

Golden syrup in jam making – golden syrup gives its special flavour to jam, but used alone it will not give a good set. You can, however, use 25% golden syrup and 75% sugar for a firm set, or 50% golden syrup and 50% sugar for a softer jam.

Stirring the sugar in jam making
You will notice that a lot of stress has been laid in the various recipes on stirring the sugar until it has dissolved. This is very important because the undissolved sugar could burn on the bottom of the pan or give you a slightly crystallised effect in the finished jam. You can always tell if the sugar is undissolved if you tap the bottom of the pan with a wooden spoon. There is a faint 'crunch' if there are any grains of sugar left.

Using acid or lemon juice in jam making
Because some fruits do not set well, you will find the juice of a lemon included in some recipes, or mention made of citric or tartaric acid. The acid can be used in place of the lemon juice. Substitute $\frac{1}{2}$ level teaspoon for 1 average sized lemon.

Amount of lemon to use in jam making
If the recipe includes the juice of a lemon, choose one of average size, which will give a good yield of juice. Should the lemon be rather dry, use a second to make certain of a set.

Scum on preserves
Most jams and jellies form a scum as they cook. It is very wasteful to try and take this off a number of times during cooking. It is better to wait until the jam has reached setting point and then give a very brisk stir which may disperse the scum. If any remains, take this off with a metal spoon. A knob of butter put in while making helps to prevent scum forming. There is nothing harmful in this, but if you are entering jam for a competition it could spoil the clarity of the preserve.

Filling jam jars
Fill your jars to about $\frac{1}{8} - \frac{1}{4}$ inch from the top. This not only saves space, but the jam will keep better. If you have any half-filled jars, use these up quickly.

Many people expect that from each pound of sugar and pound of fruit, etc. they will have 2 lb. jam, and indeed it often happens and the jam tastes delicious and keeps well.

It is, however, a proved fact today that perfect jam (by this I mean jam that will keep throughout the season) should contain 60% sugar. This means that from your pound of sugar you get less than 2 lb. jam.

In a preserve or conserve where the fruit is poached in a thick syrup, you may get a little more than $1\frac{2}{3}$ lb. jam.

With jams using commercial pectin, the yield per pound of sugar is rather more than the table below, which gives an indication of the yield.

Pounds of sugar	Final weight of jam
1 lb.	$1\frac{2}{3}$ lb.
2 lb.	$3\frac{1}{3}$ lb.
3 lb.	5 lb.
4 lb.	$6\frac{2}{3}$ lb.
5 lb.	$8\frac{1}{3}$ lb.
6 lb.	10 lb.
7 lb.	$11\frac{2}{3}$ lb.
8 lb.	$13\frac{1}{3}$ lb.

Importance of testing jam
On page 7 are the methods of testing whether your jam or jelly has set. Many people leave this testing rather late and they then find that the jam does not set. Often they think it is because it has been *under* boiled whereas in actual fact it has been boiled for such a long period that the setting point has been passed. With some fruits when once this has happened you cannot get them to set properly afterwards. The only remedy would be to mix with other well made jam.

Storing preserves

You must be careful where you store your preserves. The cupboard should be very dry. Dampness, or condensation of steam can cause the formation of mould.

If your house is centrally heated, the jam may become too dry and hard with storing. To prevent this, put your jam into proper bottling jars and you will find that it is not affected by the heat. To keep jam a good colour store away from a bright light.

Using preserves

While well made jam keeps for a very long time there will be a tendency for it to ferment if you fill only half the jar for this allows air to come into contact with the jam, in time, causing evaporation.

20 points for perfect jams, jellies and marmalades

1 Select firm – ripe – but not over-ripe fruit.
2 Follow recipe carefully for amount of sugar to fruit. Many people think all fruits need 1 lb. sugar to 1 lb. fruit – this is quite wrong. Where a fruit has little natural pectin (setting quality), i.e. sweet cherries – you need *more* fruit than sugar, and in addition it helps to add acid in the form of lemon juice, redcurrant juice, or commercial pectin.

Where a fruit is rich in pectin, e.g. blackcurrants, you get a better jam if you use more sugar than fruit.
3 Select a large enough pan, to allow jam to boil hard without splashing.
4 Use preserving, loaf or granulated sugar. Warm the sugar slightly as this will make it dissolve more quickly.
5 Do stew the fruit *slowly*. This is very important for it:
    (a) extracts pectin (natural setting substance).
    (b) softens skins – test most carefully; the skin *must* be soft before you add the sugar.
    (c) helps to keep jam a good colour.
6 Stir until sugar has dissolved, to make certain the jam does not burn or crystallise during cooking.
7 When the sugar has dissolved, boil jam RAPIDLY WITHOUT STIRRING. The quicker the jam or jelly sets, the better the yield – flavour and colour.
8 Test early for setting. Some jams are ready within 3–5 minutes, others take 10–15 minutes, or even more. Many fruits will lose their set-

qualities if boiled too long and then the jam NEVER sets.
There are several ways of testing:
Weight
The table on page 6 gives the ideal yield you should obtain from the recipes.
If you have sufficiently large and strong scales weigh the preserving pan before cooking. If you feel jam or jelly is ready, weigh again. Deduct weight of pan from total weight and if it is more than the table suggests the jam needs boiling a little longer.

Temperature
If you make a lot of jams or jellies it is worth investing in a sugar thermometer – stir round in hot jam – jam has reached setting point at 220°F – 222°F; and jelly at 220°F – 221°F.
Be careful not to put thermometer on cold surface or it will break.

Forming a skin
Put a little jam on an old saucer and allow to become quite cold, then see if it forms a skin and wrinkles when pushed with a spoon or finger.
Take pan off heat while waiting for jam to cool on saucer.

Forming a flake
Stir wooden spoon round in jam so that it becomes thoroughly coated, then allow to cool. Hold horizontally and inspect jam. If it hangs in

a firm drop or flake then it has reached setting point.

Take pan off heat while waiting for jam to cool on spoon.

9 When you are satisfied that the jam is ready, take pan off the heat, and remove the scum. If there is not much scum, most of this will disappear if stirred steadily. For competitions it is wise to remove the scum with a strainer, and then stir. When making jelly remove the scum with a strainer and by drawing a piece of *white* kitchen blotting paper quickly across the surface of the preserve.

10 For a jelly or jam that contains no whole fruit:
(a) Pour at once into *hot – dry – clean* jars. Tap jar as you fill to bring air bubbles to the surface.
Fill to at least $\frac{1}{8}$ to $\frac{1}{4}$ inch from top of jar. The jam or jelly will shrink a little as it cools. This also makes certain there is less air space in the jar and, therefore, less chance of it becoming mouldy. Jars filled to the brim also look more attractive.
(b) For a jam containing whole fruit, allow jam to cool in pan until it stiffens slightly, then stir to distribute peel or whole fruit and pour into hot jars.

11 Put on waxed circles *at once* – put final transparent cover on at once, or wait until jam is quite cold. Tie down firmly or use rubber band.

12 Store in a cool, dry *dark* place.

13 If a jam shows signs of mould, it is due to:
(a) Damp fruit.
(b) Insufficient boiling – giving too low a proportion of sugar in the finished jam.
(c) Bad storage conditions (e.g. damp).
(d) Not filling jars sufficiently or covering well.

14 If jam crystallises it is due to:
(a) Either using too much sugar in proportion to the amount of fruit, or too little sugar, which necessitated over-cooking to stiffen jam.
(b) Not stirring thoroughly to make sure sugar has dissolved before boiling.
(c) Too long cooking.

15 If jam shows signs of fermenting and has a 'winey' flavour, it is due to:

(a) Using over-ripe fruit.
(b) Bottling before the jam has reached setting point.
(c) Using too little sugar or not boiling jam sufficiently to give the right proportion of sugar in finished jam.
(d) Bad storage conditions.
(e) Not covering jars correctly.

16 If jam or jelly is hard and dry, it is due to:
(a) Over-boiling.
(b) Bad covering so that jam dries out in storage. (With central heating it is always advisable to put jam or jelly either into bottling jars or use tightly fitting caps over waxed circles – not just paper covers.)

17 If jam or jelly is syrupy and not firmly set it is because:
(a) The fruit juice was lacking in pectin (not enough natural setting quality).
(b) Not boiled sufficiently, or over-boiled. Jam which is boiled PASSED setting point gives sticky, syrupy texture.
(c) Fruit juice in jelly left too long after straining – use as soon as ready.

18 If jam or jelly is a poor colour, it is due to:
(a) Poor quality fruit.
(b) Not stewing fruit slowly enough to soften it sufficiently.
(c) Over-boiling, or boiling jam too slowly up to setting point.
(d) Storing in bright light.
(e) Using a poor quality preserving pan.

19 If jam or jelly has disappointing flavour it is because:
(a) The fruit used was too ripe or under-ripe.
(b) Too much sugar was used, giving over-sweet taste.
(c) Boiling too slowly or over-boiling, takes away fresh fruit flavour.

20 If jelly is cloudy in appearance it is because:
(a) It was badly strained – use proper jelly bag (see page 30), or several thicknesses of muslin over a hair (not wire) sieve.
(b) The pulp was *forced* through the jelly bag or muslin – allow to drip by itself without pressing or encouraging it through with a spoon.

Hints when entering jams and jellies for competitions

Marks are given for

(a) Appearance of the jar:
Is it clearly marked?
Is it filled to the top? (see point 10a in 20 points for perfect jams and jellies on page 8).
Is it neatly covered by:
  (*a*) wax circle? (the correct size).
  (*b*) top covering? (point 11).
It pays to polish jars well since this helps to make them look attractive and gives a chance for the judge to admire the colour of the jam.

(b) Contents are judged on colour – it should be bright (points 5 and 7). In the case of jellies it should be crystal clear (points 5 and 7). Where whole fruit is included, this should be well distributed (point 10b).

(c) The judge will then open jars and look at the *condition of the jam or jelly* – obviously many points are lost if jams have even faint signs of mould (point 13), if slightly sugary (points 6 and 15), or have a fermented taste (point 15).

(d) Consistency – this is important. A good jam is firm but not over-stiff (point 16), a good jelly is firm but not hard and sticky and never syrupy (points 16 and 17).

(e) Flavour – this is the most important quality of all. Read points 1, 2, 5a, 13, 14, 15, 16, and 19.
The jam or jelly should have the smell and taste of fresh fruit.
When mixing fruits try to get a good proportion of each – e.g. strawberry and rhubarb – equal proportions allows one to taste both fruits, but when mixing raspberry and rhubarb, because raspberries have a strong flavour, use a little more rhubarb.
Under the heading of flavour will come points like the taste of fruit peels or skins (point 5b). If these are tough you will lose marks.

(f) Originality – in an open class you may win if you have used a less usual recipe, so look out for new ideas.

Jams, cheeses, conserves and preserves

In this chapter you will find a very varied selection of jams of every kind.
The instructions will, I think, be easy to follow, but before making a recipe, may I suggest you read through the 20 points for perfect jam making (see page 7).
You will also find cheeses, which are based on a jam recipe; conserves and preserves, which are no more difficult to make than jams, but which enable you to make something that is a little out of the ordinary.

Making a cheese
A cheese is the name given to a preserve where all the fruit is sieved before adding the sugar. They are particularly useful in the case of fruits containing a lot of pips and stones such as blackberries or damsons. If you have a small child or someone on a gastric diet, this is the type of preserve to make. Measure the fruit pulp after cooking and sieving, and allow 1 lb. of sugar to each lb. or pint of the fruit pulp.

Rub the fruit very hard through a sieve otherwise you can waste a great deal.

Making a conserve
The difference between a conserve and jam, or a preserve, is that you add additional ingredients to give a more unusual flavour.

The method of making is, however, quite usual, and not at all difficult.

Making a preserve

The difference between a jam and a preserve is that for a jam the fruit is cooked to a purée. This light cooking will retain pieces of the fruit. In the case of a preserve, however, the fruit is purposely cooked to keep it whole. This is done in two ways:

1 By 'poaching' the fruit in a sugar and water syrup, or
2 By sprinkling the sugar over the fruit and stewing gently.

Note

Do not expect the syrup in most preserves to set, as firmly as in a jam.

Apples in jam making

While most cooking apples are good in jam making, a rather cheap apple such as a Bramley Seedling retains most of its flavour. The weight given in these recipes is after peeling and coring. The peel, core and pips can be tied in muslin and simmered together with the fruit, for these give flavour and help the jam to set.

Apple and cherry jam

cooking time: 30 minutes

you will need:

| 1 lb. cooking apples (after peeling and coring) | 2¼ lb. ripe dessert cherries |
| ¼ pint water | 3 lb. sugar |

1 Simmer the apples with the water until they start to get soft.
2 Add the cherries and continue cooking until these are softened but unbroken.
3 Remove as many stones as possible.
4 Add sugar and stir until dissolved.
5 Boil rapidly until set.

Apple ginger jam (1)

cooking time: 30 minutes

you will need:

| 1 lb. cooking apples (after peeling and coring) | 1 lb. sugar |
| | 1 teaspoon ground ginger |

1 Cut the apples into neat cubes.
2 Sprinkle over the sugar.
3 Tie cores and peelings in a muslin bag, and place this in with the apples and sugar. Leave to stand overnight.
4 Put into a saucepan or preserving pan.
5 Simmer gently, stirring all the time, until the sugar has quite dissolved.
6 Add ginger.
7 Boil steadily until the cubes of apples look transparent and the syrup has set.
8 Remove cores and peel.

Apple ginger jam (2)

cooking time: 30 minutes

you will need:

| 2½ lb. cooking apples (after peeling and coring) | 1–2 teaspoons powdered ginger |
| ½ pint water | 2 lb. sugar |

1 Peel and core the apples.
2 Tie peel and cores in muslin bag.
3 Simmer the fruit with the water and ginger until a very smooth pulp. Remove muslin bag.
4 Add the sugar, and stir until dissolved.
5 Boil steadily until set.

Apple lemon jam (1)

cooking time: 30 minutes

you will need:

| 2 lb. cooking apples (after peeling and coring) | grated rind and juice of 2 lemons |
| ½ pint water | 2 lb. sugar |

1 Simmer the apples with the water and grated rind of the lemons.
2 When quite soft add lemon juice and sugar.
3 Stir until the sugar has dissolved.
4 Boil rapidly until set.

Apple lemon jam (2)

cooking time: 20–25 minutes

you will need:

2 lb. apples (after peeling and coring) grated rind 2 lemons	½ pint water 2¼ lb. sugar

1 Slice apples thinly and simmer with lemon rind and water until soft.
2 Stir in sugar and lemon juice, until sugar is dissolved.
3 Boil until set.

Apple orange jam

cooking time: 30 minutes

you will need:

2 lb. cooking apples (after peeling and coring) ½ pint water	grated rind 3 oranges pulp 3 oranges 2¼ lb. sugar

1 Simmer the apples with the water and grated orange rind.
2 When quite soft add the pulp and juice of the oranges and sugar.
3 Stir until the sugar has dissolved.
4 Boil rapidly until set.

Apple and pineapple jam

cooking time: 35 minutes

you will need:

1 lb. cooking apples (after peeling and coring) 1 lb. pineapple (weight after peeling)	⅛ pint water 2 lb. sugar

1 Dice fruit.
2 Simmer the apples and pineapple with the water until soft.
3 Stir in the sugar until dissolved.
4 Boil rapidly until set.

Apple date preserve

cooking time: 30 minutes

you will need:

2 lb. cooking apples (after peeling and coring)	juice 2 lemons 2 lb. sugar 12 oz. dessert dates

1 Peel the apples and cut the fruit into neat slices.

2 Leave for several hours with the lemon juice and sugar.
3 Put into preserving pan.
4 Stir over low heat until sugar has dissolved.
5 Add the quartered dates and continue cooking until jam has set.

Apple and plum jam

cooking time: 30 minutes

you will need:

1 lb. cooking apples (after peeling and coring) 2 lb. plums (after stoning)	¼ pint water 3 lb. sugar

1 Simmer the fruit with the water until soft.
2 Stir in sugar until dissolved.
3 Boil until set.

Apple and rhubarb jam

cooking time: 30 minutes

you will need:

1 lb. rhubarb 1 lb. cooking apples	⅛ pint water 2 lb. sugar

1 Dice the rhubarb and chop the apples.
2 Put into a saucepan with the water and simmer until soft.
3 Add the sugar, stir until dissolved.
4 Boil rapidly until set.

Apple cheeses

cooking time: 30 minutes

Any of the apple jam or preserve recipes can be made into a cheese.

1 Simmer the fruit and water until soft.
2 Rub through a sieve and measure the pulp.
3 Allow 1 lb. sugar to each 1 lb. or pint of pulp.
4 Stir until the sugar has dissolved.
5 Boil rapidly until set.

Note
There is no need to peel or core the apples.

Apple and damson jam

cooking time: 30 minutes

you will need:

1 lb. cooking apples (after peeling and coring)	½ pint water
	2¼ lb. sugar
1½ lb. damsons (stoned)	

1 Put the fruits with the water into a pan.
2 Simmer until soft.
3 Remove as many damson stones as possible.
4 Stir in the sugar.
5 Boil rapidly until set.
   This jam will be enjoyed by the people who find damsons rather 'biting'.

Apple fig preserve

cooking time: 30 minutes

you will need:

2 lb. cooking apples (after peeling and coring)	2 lb. sugar
	¼ pint water
juice 2 lemons	8 oz. dried figs

1 Peel the apples and cut the fruit into neat slices.
2 Leave for several hours with the lemon juice, sugar, and water.
3 Put into preserving pan.
4 Stir over low heat until sugar has dissolved.
5 Add the dried figs cut into neat fingers and continue cooking until jam has set.

Apricot jam

cooking time: 30 minutes

you will need:

1 lb. fresh apricots	1 lb. sugar
2–3 tablespoons water (if fruit is under-ripe, use ⅛ pint)	¼ level teaspoon citric or tartaric acid or juice ½ lemon

1 Cut the fruit into pieces.
2 If desired, crack the stones and take out the kernels.
3 Put into preserving pan with the water and simmer until the fruit is soft.

4 Add the sugar and lemon juice or acid and stir until dissolved.
5 Boil rapidly until set.

Apricot conserve

cooking time: 35 minutes

you will need:

1 lb. ripe apricots	1 lb. sugar
juice 1 lemon	

1 Halve small apricots or quarter large ones.
2 Put into the pan with the lemon juice and sugar.
3 Heat very gently, stirring all the time until the sugar has dissolved.
4 Boil steadily until set.

Apricot and almond conserve

cooking time: 30 minutes

Use apricot jam recipe, but add 2 oz. blanched chopped almonds when jam has set.

Apricot jam (dried fruit)

cooking time: 1¼ hours

you will need:

1 lb. dried apricots	1½ level teaspoons citric or tartaric acid, or juice 2 lemons
3 pints water	
3 lb. sugar	

1 Soak the fruit in the water for 48 or even 72 hours.
2 Simmer gently until the fruit is soft.
3 Add the sugar and acid or lemon juice, stir until dissolved.
4 Boil rapidly until set.

Apricot conserve (dried fruit)

cooking time: 1½–2 hours

1 Follow the recipe for dried apricot jam (see above), and allow 2 oranges and 2 oz. seedless raisins to each lb. dried apricots.
2 Soak the slices of orange with the apricots, tying the pips in a muslin bag.
3 Add the dried fruit to the apricots and oranges.

4 Simmer until soft.

5 Remove the pips and continue as for dried apricot jam.

6 When this has reached setting point, add 2 oz. chopped walnuts or brazils.

Apricot and cherry jam

cooking time: 30 minutes

you will need:

2 lb. apricots	3 lb. sugar
1 lb. cherries	juice 2 lemons
¼ pint water (if fruit is very firm, use ½ pint water)	

1 Simmer the fruit with the water until soft.

2 Add the sugar and the lemon juice.

3 Stir until the sugar is dissolved.

4 Boil rapidly until set.

Banana and apple jam

cooking time: 30 minutes

you will need:

1 lb. cooking apples (after peeling and coring)	grated rind 2 lemons
	2 lb. bananas
	juice 2 lemons
¼ pint water	3 lb. sugar

1 Simmer the apples with the water and lemon rind.

2 When soft, add the mashed banana and lemon juice.

3 Cook for a few minutes only.

4 Add the sugar and stir until dissolved.

5 Boil rapidly until set.

Banana and lemon jam

cooking time: 1¼ hours

you will need:

6 bananas	1 lb. castor sugar
3 lemons	

1 Peel and cut up the bananas as small as possible.

2 Grate the lemon rind and squeeze and strain the juice.

3 Put the bananas, grated rind and juice in a china or glass bowl.

4 Cover with the sugar.

5 Allow to stand for 1 hour for the sugar to dissolve.

6 Place the contents of the bowl into a pan and bring very slowly to the boil. This should take about 1 hour.

7 Boil until the jam sets.

Banana and orange jam

cooking time: 1¼ hours

you will need:

6 bananas	1 lb. castor sugar
3 oranges	

1 Peel and slice bananas.

2 Put into preserving pan.

3 Pour the strained juice over, and add grated rind and pulp of the oranges.

4 Add the sugar.

5 Leave to stand for 30 minutes.

6 Bring to the boil very slowly.

7 Boil rapidly until set.

Blackberry jam

cooking time: 25 minutes

you will need:

2 lb. blackberries	sugar
juice 1 lemon	

1 Simmer fruit and lemon juice.

2 Sieve to remove pips.

3 Allow 1 lb. sugar to each pint pulp.

4 Reheat fruit.

5 Stir in sugar until dissolved, and boil steadily until set.

Blackberry cheese

cooking time: 30 minutes

you will need:

1 lb. cooking apples (unpeeled)	¼ pint water
2 lb. blackberries	sugar

1 Simmer the sliced apples, blackberries and water until soft.

2 Rub through a sieve and measure the pulp.

3 Allow 1 lb. sugar to each lb. or pint of the pulp.

4 Stir until the sugar has dissolved.

5 Boil rapidly until set.

Blackberry and apple jam

cooking time: 25–30 minutes

you will need:

1 lb. cooking apples (after peeling and coring)	⅛ pint water
	1 lb. blackberries
	2 lb. sugar

1 Put the sliced apples and water into the preserving pan.
2 Cook gently until the apples become soft.
3 Add the blackberries.
4 Continue cooking until all the fruit is soft.
5 Stir in the sugar.
6 Continue stirring until sugar is dissolved.
7 Boil rapidly until jam has set.

Blackberry and elderberry jam

cooking time: 25–30 minutes

you will need:

1 lb. blackberries	2 lb. sugar
1 lb. elderberries	juice 2 lemons

1 Simmer the fruit until soft. There should be no need to add water unless the fruit is very under-ripe.
2 Stir in the sugar and lemon juice.
3 Boil rapidly until set.

Blackberry and pineapple jam

cooking time: approximately 35–40 minutes

you will need:

1 lb. fresh pineapple (peeled)	1 lb. blackberries
2 large cooking apples, peeled and cored	3 lb. sugar
little water	juice 3 lemons

1 Dice pineapple and mix with slices of apple.
2 Simmer gently for about 15 minutes adding as little water as possible.
3 Add the blackberries and continue cooking for a further 5–10 minutes until soft.
4 Stir in the sugar and the lemon juice, and stir until sugar is dissolved.
5 Boil rapidly until set.

The secret of tender blackcurrants in jam

1 Simmer the fruit very gently – and *never* add sugar until you are certain the fruit is tender.
2 After cooking gently for about 15–20 minutes, try one or two currants. The skin should be so soft you can nearly 'rub it away' with your fingers.

Blackcurrant jam (1)

cooking time: 40 minutes

you will need:

1 lb. blackcurrants	1¼ lb. sugar
¾ pint water	

1 Put the fruit and water into preserving pan.
2 Simmer very slowly until the blackcurrants are quite soft.
3 Stir in the sugar.
4 Boil rapidly until set.

Blackcurrant jam (2)

Use recipe and method as Blackcurrant jam (1) but use only ½ pint water. This gives a thicker jam with a stronger flavour.

Blackcurrant and apple jam

cooking time: 40 minutes

you will need:

1 lb. blackcurrants	1 lb. cooking apples (after peeling and coring)
½ pint water	2¼ lb. sugar

1 Simmer the blackcurrants and water for approximately 15 minutes.
2 Add the sliced apples and continue cooking until soft.
3 Stir in the sugar, and stir until dissolved.
4 Boil rapidly until set.

Blackcurrant and rhubarb jam

cooking time: 40 minutes

you will need:

1 lb. blackcurrants	1 lb. rhubarb, sliced
½ pint water	2¼ lb. sugar

1 Simmer the blackcurrants and water for approximately 15 minutes.
2 Add the rhubarb and continue cooking until soft.
3 Add the sugar and stir until dissolved.
4 Boil rapidly until set.

Blackcurrant cheeses

cooking time: 30 minutes

Because many people find the pips of blackcurrants rather troublesome, a cheese made from this fruit is very delicious. Use any of the recipes. Rub through a sieve. If you like a rather sharp jam, use only 14 oz. sugar to each pint of pulp. Most people will like just over a lb. of sugar to each pint or lb. of pulp.

Blackcurrant and redcurrant jam (1)

cooking time: 35–40 minutes

you will need:

1 lb. blackcurrants	¾ pint water
1 lb. redcurrants	2¼ lb. sugar

1 Simmer fruit with water until skins become very soft.
2 Add the sugar and stir until sugar is dissolved. Bring to the boil rapidly.
3 Test very soon after boiling point is reached, as this jam sets very quickly.

Blackcurrant and redcurrant jam (2)

cooking time: 40 minutes

you will need:

2 lb. blackcurrants	1 lb. redcurrants
1¼ pints water	3 lb. sugar

Use method for blackcurrant jam (1) but simmer blackcurrants with water for 10 minutes, then add redcurrants.

Blaeberry jam

This is another name for blueberries, see below.

Bilberry jam

This is another name for blueberries, see below.

Whortleberry jam

This is another name for blueberries, see below.

Blueberry jam

cooking time: 20 minutes

you will need:

1 lb. blueberries	1 lb. sugar

1 Simmer the fruit for 5 minutes only, using no water.
2 Add the sugar and stir until dissolved.
3 Boil steadily until just set.

Note
This jam sets quickly and boiling too rapidly will spoil the shape of the blueberries.

Black cherry preserve

cooking time: 35 minutes

you will need:

1¼ lb. black cherries	1 lb. sugar
	juice 1 lemon

1 Sprinkle the sugar over the cherries and leave to stand for several hours.
2 Put into the pan with the lemon juice and simmer gently until the sugar has dissolved, stirring well.
3 Boil rapidly until a little of the syrup is fairly firm.

Note
This jam should never be very stiff.

15

Cherry jam

cooking time: 20–25 minutes

you will need:

1 lb. cherries* (stoned) or nearly 1¼ lb. before stoning 12 oz. sugar	juice ½ lemon or ¼ level teaspoon citric or tartaric acid

*If using red morello cherries use only half the quantity of acid. Use black cherries for Swiss jam.

1 Tie the stones in muslin, and add to the fruit in the pan.
2 Simmer until the skin of the fruit is soft.
3 Stir in the sugar, and add lemon juice or acid.
4 Continue stirring until sugar is dissolved.
5 Boil rapidly until set.

Cherry conserve

cooking time: 20–25 minutes

1 Use recipe and method for cherry jam, but add 2 oz. raisins to each lb. cherries and simmer these with the fruit.
2 When jam has reached setting point, add 2 oz. chopped walnuts to each lb. fruit.

Cherry and apricot jam

cooking time: 25 minutes

you will need:

1 lb. stoned morello or red cherries* 1 lb. fresh apricots (stoned)	¼ pint water 2 lb. sugar juice 2 lemons

*Use just over 1 lb. if you want to remove stones as they rise to the top during cooking.

1 Put the fruit and water into pan and simmer gently until tender.
2 Add sugar and lemon juice, and stir until sugar is dissolved.
3 Boil steadily until set.

Clove and apple jam

cooking time: 30 minutes

1 Use recipe and method for apple ginger jam (see page 10) but omit ginger and allow 3–4 cloves per lb. of jam.

2 Tie cloves in muslin and remove when jam has set.

Cranberry jam

cooking time: 35 minutes

you will need:

1 lb. cranberries ¼ pint water	1¼ lb. sugar

1 Simmer the cranberries with the water until skins are soft. If the fruit is very firm you may need to add a little extra water.
2 Add the sugar and stir until dissolved.
3 Boil rapidly until set.

Cranberry conserve

cooking time: 35 minutes

1 Use the recipe and method for cranberry jam (see above), adding grated rind of 1 orange and 2 oz. currants to each lb. of cranberries.
2 When setting point is reached, add 2 oz. blanched chopped almonds to each lb. of conserve.

Cucumber jam

cooking time: 30 minutes

you will need:

2 lb. cucumber (after peeling) ¼ pint water	juice 2 lemons 2 lb. sugar

1 Simmer the diced cucumber in the water until soft.
2 Add the lemon juice and sugar.
3 Stir until sugar has dissolved.
4 Boil rapidly until set.

Variation

With colouring – this jam tends to be a little pale in colour and you may like to add a few drops of green colouring. Or you can simmer the cucumber with a little of the peel left on and rub it through a sieve. The peel helps to give a cool green colour: too much peel will give the jam a bitter taste.

Cucumber and ginger jam

cooking time: 30 minutes

Use the recipe and method as cucumber jam, adding a little powdered ginger to taste.

Damson jam

cooking time: 25–30 minutes

you will need:

¼ pint water (if fruit   1 lb. damsons
  is ripe)   1 lb. sugar

If fruit is very under-ripe, use the following quantities:

1 lb. damsons   1¼ lb. sugar
¼ pint water

1 Put the fruit and water into a preserving pan.
2 Simmer until soft, removing as many stones as possible.
3 Add sugar and stir until dissolved.
4 Boil rapidly until set.

Damson cheeses

cooking time: 30 minutes

As it takes such a long time to remove the stones from damson jam, a cheese is a very good way of avoiding this. Use any of the damson jam recipes. Rub the fruit through a sieve. Allow 1 lb. of sugar to each lb. or pint of pulp. Stir until the sugar has dissolved and boil rapidly until set.

Damson and marrow jam

cooking time: 35–40 minutes

you will need:

1 lb. damsons   ¼ pint water
1 lb. marrow (peeled)   2 lb. sugar

1 Put damsons, diced marrow and water into a preserving pan.
2 Simmer until soft.
3 Remove as many stones as possible.
4 Add the sugar and stir until dissolved.
5 Boil rapidly until set.

Elderberry jam

cooking time: 25 minutes

you will need:

1 lb. elderberries   juice 1 lemon
1 lb. sugar

1 Crush the elderberries in preserving pan.
2 Simmer until soft.
3 Add the sugar and stir well until dissolved.
4 Add lemon juice.
5 Boil rapidly until set.

Elderberry and apple jam

cooking time: 30 minutes

you will need:

1 lb. elderberries   ¼ pint water
1 lb. apples   2 lb. sugar

1 Simmer the fruit with the water until tender.
2 Add the sugar and stir until dissolved.
3 Boil rapidly until set.

Fresh fig preserve

cooking time: 45 minutes

you will need:

1 lb. fresh ripe figs   juice 1 lemon
1 lb. sugar

1 If the figs are very small, they can be left whole. If large, halve or quarter them.
2 Put into the preserving pan with the sugar and lemon juice.
3 Heat gently, stirring all the time until the sugar has dissolved.
4 Boil steadily until set.

Green fig preserve

cooking time: 45 minutes

Use recipe and method for fresh fig preserve, using green figs.

Fig and lemon jam

cooking time: 1–1¼ hours

you will need:

2 lb. dried figs	3 lb. sugar
1½ pints water	juice 2 lemons

1 Soak figs in water for 12 hours.
2 Rinse in fresh water.
3 Cut into small pieces, removing any hard pieces of stem.
4 Put into a preserving pan with 1½ pints fresh hot water.
5 Simmer until tender.
6 Stir in sugar and strained lemon juice.
7 Continue to cook, until the preserve is thick.
8 Pour into jam jars while hot.

Four fruit jam

cooking time: 20–25 minutes

you will need:

8 oz. blackcurrants	8 oz. raspberries
¼ pint water	8 oz. strawberries
8 oz. redcurrants	2 lb. sugar

1 Simmer blackcurrants in the water until nearly soft.
2 Add the rest of the fruit.
3 Continue cooking for a further 5–10 minutes.
4 Add the sugar, stirring until dissolved.
5 Boil rapidly until set.

Fruit salad jam (dried fruit)

cooking time: 1¼ hours

Use recipe and method for dried apricot jam but substitute dried fruit salad.
The taste of this jam is most pleasant.

Gooseberries in jam making

People are often disappointed with the colour of their gooseberry jam. If you want a really green jam, then you must use the firm green fruit. Ripe gooseberries, even if they have not turned red, give a pinky coloured jam.

Gooseberry jam

cooking time: 25–35 minutes

you will need:

1 lb. gooseberries	1 lb. sugar
¼ pint water (if fruit is ripe)	

If fruit is very under-ripe use the following quantities:

1 lb. gooseberries	1¼ lb. sugar
½ pint water	

1 Put the fruit and water into a preserving pan.
2 Simmer until soft.
3 Add the sugar and stir until dissolved.
4 Boil rapidly until set.

Gooseberry and cherry jam

cooking time: 25–30 minutes

you will need:

1 lb. firm gooseberries	1¼ lb. cherries
¼ pint water	2 lb. sugar

1 Put the gooseberries, water and cherries into the preserving pan.
2 Simmer until soft, removing as many cherry stones as possible.
3 Add sugar and stir until dissolved.
4 Boil until set.

Gooseberry and loganberry jam

cooking time: 25 minutes

you will need:

1 lb. ripe gooseberries	1 lb. loganberries
¼ pint water	2 lb. sugar

1 Simmer the gooseberries with the water for about 10 minutes.
2 Add loganberries and continue cooking until these are soft.
3 Add sugar and stir until dissolved.
4 Boil rapidly until set.

Gooseberry and orange jam

cooking time: 25–35 minutes

you will need:

1¼ lb. gooseberries	2 oranges
¼ pint water	1½ lb. sugar

1 Simmer gooseberries gently until tender with water, orange juice, and grated orange rind.

2 Add sugar and stir until dissolved.
3 Boil until setting point is reached.

Gooseberry and rhubarb conserve

cooking time: 30 minutes

you will need:

1 lb. rhubarb   2 lb. sugar
1 lb. gooseberries   juice 1 lemon

1 Cut the rhubarb into pieces about $\frac{1}{2}$ inch in length.
2 Put into the pan with the gooseberries, sugar and lemon juice.
3 Leave to stand for several hours.
4 Heat gently, stirring all the time until the sugar has dissolved.
5 Boil rapidly until the jam has set lightly.

Gooseberry and strawberry jam

cooking time: 25 minutes

you will need:

1 lb. ripe gooseberries   1 lb. ripe strawberries
$\frac{1}{4}$ pint water   2 lb. sugar

1 Simmer the gooseberries with the water for about 10 minutes.
2 Add the strawberries and continue cooking until these are soft.
3 Add sugar and stir until dissolved.
4 Boil rapidly until set.

Gooseberry and strawberry conserve

cooking time: 30 minutes

you will need:

1 lb. strawberries   2 lb. sugar
1 lb. gooseberries   juice 1 lemon

1 Leave the strawberries whole and put into the pan with the gooseberries, sugar and lemon juice.
2 Leave to stand for several hours.
3 Heat gently, stirring all the time until the sugar has dissolved.
4 Boil rapidly until the jam has set lightly.

Gooseberry cheeses

cooking time: 30 minutes

Any of the gooseberry jam recipes will make a good cheese. As you will sieve the fruit for this, there is no need to 'top and tail' the gooseberries. Rub the fruit through a sieve. Allow 1 lb. of sugar to each pint or lb. of pulp. Boil rapidly until set.

Greengage jam

cooking time: 20–25 minutes

you will need:

1 lb. greengages   use no water if fruit is
(stoned)   ripe ($\frac{1}{8}$ pint water if
                      under-ripe)
                      1 lb. sugar

1 The stones of the fruit can be cracked and the kernels included.
2 Simmer fruit until soft, adding water if necessary.
3 Add sugar and stir until dissolved.
4 Boil rapidly until set, adding kernels at the last minute.

Greengage and apple jam

cooking time: 35 minutes

you will need:

2 lb. greengages $\frac{1}{4}$ pint water
(stoned)   3 lb. sugar
1 lb. cooking apples
(after peeling and
coring)

1 Simmer the fruit until soft. If the greengages are very ripe, they can be added after the apples have started to cook.
2 Add sugar and stir until dissolved.
3 Boil until set.

Greengage and red plum jam

cooking time: 25 minutes

you will need:

1 lb. greengages   2 lb. sugar
(stoned) $\frac{1}{8}$ pint water
1 lb. red plums
(stoned)

Use recipe and method as for greengage jam.

Green grape jam

cooking time: 15–20 minutes

you will need:

1 lb. sharp green grapes	1 lb. sugar

1 Simmer the fruit, for a few minutes, using no water unless necessary.
2 Add sugar and stir until dissolved.
3 Boil rapidly until set.

Black grape jam

cooking time: 15–20 minutes

you will need:

1 lb. black grapes juice 2 lemons	1 lb. sugar

Use method for green grape jam, adding the lemon juice with the sugar.

Grape cheese

cooking time: 15–20 minutes

Since many do not like the pips and skin of grapes in a jam, simmer fruit until soft and then rub through a sieve. Allow 1 lb. sugar to each pint or lb. of pulp and if grapes are ripe add the juice of 1 lemon. Stir until sugar has dissolved. Boil rapidly until set.

Guava jam

cooking time: 25–30 minutes

you will need:

1 lb. guava pulp ¼ pint water	1 lb. sugar juice 1 lemon

1 Simmer the pulp with the water until very soft.
2 Stir in the sugar and lemon juice.
3 Stir until sugar has dissolved.
4 Boil rapidly until set.

Huckleberry jam

cooking time: 25 minutes

you will need:

1 lb. huckleberries* water	2 lb. sugar juice 2 lemons

*Blueberries can be used instead.

1 Simmer the huckleberries with very little water.

2 Add sugar and lemon juice, stir until the sugar dissolves.
3 Boil until set.

Variation

With apples – if preferred you may use: 1 lb. huckleberries, 1 lb. cooking apples (after peeling and coring) and 2 lb. sugar. As huckleberries are lacking in pectin, you MUST put something in to help the jam to set.

Japonica jam

cooking time: 40 minutes

you will need:

1 lb. japonica (unpeeled) 1–1¼ pints water (depending on ripeness of fruit)	pinch ground ginger 2 lemons sugar

1 Do not peel or core the japonica.
2 Cut into halves and simmer in the water until pulp.
3 Add ground ginger.
4 Sieve and to each pint or lb. of pulp, add lemon juice and 1 lb. sugar.
5 Stir in the sugar until dissolved.
6 Boil until set.

Lemon and melon jam

cooking time: 30 minutes

you will need:

1 lb. melon (after peeling) 1 lb. sugar	grated rind and juice 2 lemons

1 Dice the melon.
2 Allow to stand overnight, with the sugar.
3 Next day put into a preserving pan.
4 Simmer gently, stirring well until the sugar has dissolved.
5 Add the lemon juice, and lemon rind.
6 Boil steadily until set.

Loganberry jam

cooking time: 20 minutes

you will need:

1 lb. loganberries	1 lb. sugar

1 Simmer fruit until soft.

2 Add sugar and stir until dissolved.
3 Boil rapidly until set.

Loganberry and cherry jam

cooking time: 25 minutes

you will need:

1 lb. cherries*   2 lb. sugar
1 lb. loganberries

*If cherries are very ripe, allow 1¼ lb. cherries.

1 Simmer fruit until soft, removing as many cherry stones as possible.
2 Add sugar and stir until dissolved.
3 Boil rapidly until set.

Loganberry and raspberry jam

cooking time: 20 minutes

you will need:

1 lb. loganberries   2 lb. sugar
1 lb. raspberries

1 Simmer loganberries until nearly soft.
2 Add raspberries and cook for a further few minutes.
3 Add sugar and stir until dissolved.
4 Boil rapidly until set.

Loganberry and redcurrant jam

cooking time: 20 minutes

you will need:

1 lb. loganberries   ¼ pint water
1 lb. redcurrants   2 lb. sugar

Use method for loganberry jam.

Loganberry cheeses

cooking time: 20-25 minutes

you will need:

Use any of the recipes for loganberry jam, but rub through a sieve. Allow 1 lb. sugar to 1 lb. or pint fruit purée. Boil rapidly until set.

Lychee jam (fresh fruit)

cooking time: 15 minutes

you will need:

1 lb. fresh lychees   Just under 1 lb. sugar
(when removed   juice 1 lemon
from their shells)

1 Simmer the lychees with the sugar and lemon juice. Remove stones.
2 Stir well until sugar has dissolved.
3 Boil steadily until set.

Lychee preserve (canned fruit)

cooking time: 15 minutes

1 Drain off syrup from can of lychees.
2 Weigh the fruit and allow 8 oz. sugar to each 1 lb. fruit.
3 Simmer the syrup from the tin with the extra sugar until this has dissolved.
4 Boil rapidly for a few minutes until a thicker syrup is formed.
5 Put in the lychees and simmer steadily for about 10 minutes.
6 If a firmer syrup is desired, add the juice of another lemon with a little extra sugar.

Marrow in jam making

The best flavoured marrow for jam is the late vegetable; a large marrow gives the best result.

Marrow and ginger jam

cooking time: 20-30 minutes

you will need:

1 lb. marrow (after   1 level teaspoon
peeling), cut into   ground ginger, or
cubes   1-2 oz. crystallised
1 lb. sugar   ginger
                          juice 1 large lemon

Use method for apple ginger jam (see page 10).

Marrow and lemon jam

cooking time: 25 minutes

you will need:

1 lb. marrow (after peeling), cut into cubes

juice and grated rind 2 lemons
1 lb. sugar

1 Put the marrow, lemon rind and sugar together and leave to stand overnight.
2 Simmer gently, adding lemon juice and stirring well until sugar has dissolved.
3 Boil steadily until set.

Marrow and orange jam

cooking time: 25 minutes

you will need:

1 lb. marrow (after peeling), cut into cubes
1 lb. sugar

pulp and grated rind 2 oranges
juice 1 lemon

Use the method for marrow and lemon jam, adding orange rind, orange pulp and lemon juice.

Melon and ginger jam

cooking time: 30 minutes

you will need:

1 lb. melon (after peeling)
1–2 oz. crystallised ginger

1 lb. sugar
juice 2 lemons

1 Dice melon.
2 Cut the crystallised ginger into small pieces.
3 Allow the melon, sugar and ginger to stand overnight.
4 Put into preserving pan and simmer gently, stirring until sugar has dissolved.
5 Add the lemon juice.
6 Boil steadily until set.

Mulberry jam (1)

cooking time: 30 minutes

you will need:

1 lb. mulberries
$\frac{1}{8}$ pint water

1 lb. sugar

1 Simmer the fruit with the water until soft.
2 Add sugar and stir until dissolved.
3 Boil rapidly until set.

Mulberry jam (2)

cooking time: 30 minutes

you will need:

1 lb. mulberries
8 oz. cooking apples (after peeling and coring)

$\frac{1}{4}$ pint water
1 lb. sugar

1 Mix mulberries, apples and water in a preserving pan.
2 Simmer together until tender.
3 Rub through a sieve.
4 Add sugar to the pulp, and stir until dissolved.
5 Boil rapidly until set.

Mulberry cheese

cooking time: 35 minutes

you will need:

mulberries
water

sugar

Because mulberries are so 'woody' in the centre it is even better to make a cheese.
1 To each lb. fruit, allow $\frac{1}{8}$ pint water.
2 Simmer steadily until soft, rub through sieve.
3 Allow 1 lb. sugar to each pint or lb. of pulp.
4 Stir well, adding the sugar.
5 Stir until sugar has dissolved.
6 Boil rapidly until set.

Passion fruit jam (fresh fruit) (1)

cooking time: 15 minutes

If the passion fruit is very ripe, allow the juice of 1 lemon to each pint of pulp.

1 Scoop out the pulp and allow 1 lb. sugar to 1 pint pulp.
2 Simmer the pulp with the sugar, stirring well until dissolved.
3 Boil rapidly until set.

Passion fruit jam (canned fruit) (2)

cooking time: approximately 15 minutes

Use canned passion fruit pulp. If sweetened allow 8 oz. sugar to each pint of pulp.
Use method for passion fruit jam (1).

Peach jam

cooking time: 30 minutes

Use recipe and method for apricot jam (see page 12).
Small under-ripe home-grown fruit could be used, in which case allow $\frac{1}{4}$ pint water to each lb. of fruit.

Peach conserve

cooking time: 35 minutes

you will need:

1 lb. ripe peaches   1 lb. sugar
juice 1 lemon

1 Halve small peaches or quarter large ones.
2 Put into the pan with the lemon juice and sugar.
3 Heat very gently, stirring all the time until the sugar has dissolved.
4 Boil steadily until set.

Peach jam (dried fruit)

cooking time: 1¼–1½ hours

Use recipe and method for apricot jam using dried fruit, see page 12, but use dried peaches instead.

Peach conserve (dried fruit)

cooking time: 1½ hours

1 Follow the recipe for dried peach jam (see above) and allow 1 lb. dried peaches, and 2 oz. seedless raisins to 2 oranges.
2 Soak the slices of orange with the peaches, tying the pips in a muslin bag.
3 Add the dried fruit to the peaches and oranges.
4 Simmer until soft.
5 Remove the pips and continue as for peach jam.
6 When setting point is reached add 2 oz. chopped almonds to each lb. of jam.

Peach and pear jam

cooking time: 30–35 minutes

you will need:

1 lb. ripe firm pears   ¼ pint water
  (after peeling and   2 lb. sugar
  coring)   juice and grated rind
1 lb. peaches   2 lemons

1 Cut the pears into neat cubes and quarter the peaches.
2 Simmer gently with the water until soft, but do not reduce to a pulp.
3 Stir in the sugar and lemon rind and juice.
4 Stir until sugar has dissolved and boil rapidly until set.

Peach and pear conserve

cooking time: 30 minutes

Use ingredients as for peach and pear jam.
1 Boil sugar, water and lemon rind together for about 5 minutes until it becomes a thick syrup.
2 Add the pieces of fruit with the lemon juice and simmer steadily until these are transparent. The syrup should be thick to set firmly.

Pear and clove jam

cooking time: 30-45 minutes

Use recipe and method as for clove and apple jam (see page 16), using firm cooking pears instead of apples.

Pear and ginger jam

cooking time: 30-45 minutes

Use recipe and method as for apple ginger jam (see page 10), using firm pears instead of apples.

Note

If very hard pears are used, you may need a little extra water and a further 15 minutes cooking time.

Pear and lemon jam

cooking time: 30-45 minutes

Use recipe and method as for apple lemon jam (see page 10), using firm pears instead of apples.

Note

If very hard pears are used, you may need a little extra water and a further 15 minutes cooking time.

Pear and pineapple conserve

cooking time: 45 minutes

you will need:

3 lb. pears	sugar
1 medium can	¼ pint bottle
small pineapple cubes	maraschino cherries
1 orange	

1 Cut pears into ½-inch cubes.
2 Add the pineapple, grated rind and orange juice.

3 Weigh the fruits and to each lb. add 12 oz. sugar.
4 Leave to stand overnight in a bowl.
5 Place in a preserving pan and simmer until thick.
6 Cut the cherries in half.
7 Add cherries and liquid from the bottle to the fruit.
8 Stir well but do not re-cook.
9 Pour into wide necked bottle and seal at once.

Pear preserve

cooking time: 25–30 minutes

you will need:

1 lb. ripe pears	½ pint water
1 lb. sugar	juice 2 lemons

1 Peel and cut the pears into neat pieces.
2 Simmer the sugar and water until the sugar has dissolved.
3 Add the pears and the lemon juice.
4 Cook slowly until these are soft.

Pear and ginger preserve

cooking time: 25–30 minutes

you will need:

1 lb. ripe pears	½ pint water
2 oz. preserved ginger	juice 2 lemons
1 lb. sugar	

1 Peel and cut the pears into neat pieces, together with the preserved ginger.
2 Simmer the sugar and water until the sugar has dissolved.
3 Add the pears, ginger and lemon juice.
4 Cook slowly until tender.

Pear and orange jam

cooking time: 30–45 minutes

Use recipe as for apple orange jam (see page 11), using pears instead of apples.

Note

If very hard pears are used, you may need a little extra water and a further 15 minutes cooking time.

Plums in jam making

Many people are inclined to use over-ripe plums in jam.

For a perfect flavour they should be firm, ripe, but not too soft.

Do not worry if there is a slight 'waxy' substance round the stone of the plum – that is completely harmless.

It is worth mixing plums with other kinds of fruit; each will give distinctive flavour.

Plum jam (1)

cooking time: 20–25 minutes

you will need:

1 lb. plums (stoned)	use no water if fruit is ripe ($\frac{1}{8}$ pint if under-ripe)
1 lb. sugar	

Use method as for greengage jam (see page 19).

Plum jam (2)

cooking time: 25–30 minutes

If whole fruit jam is required, proceed as follows:

1 Cut plums into halves. Remove the stones.
2 Put into a bowl and sprinkle with the sugar.
3 Leave to stand overnight.
4 The next day proceed as usual, simmering until sugar has dissolved.
5 Boil *steadily* until set.

Plum jam (3)

cooking time: 20–25 minutes

you will need:

1 lb. plums (stoned)	use no water if fruit is ripe ($\frac{1}{8}$ pint if under-ripe)
12 oz. sugar	

1 Simmer the plums with the water, if used, until fruit is soft.
2 Add sugar and stir until dissolved.
3 Boil rapidly until set.

Note

This gives a very good flavour for people who do not like jam which is very sweet, but it may not keep so well and it should be used fairly rapidly.

Plum conserve

cooking time: 20 minutes

1 Use recipe for any of the plum jams (see before), but allow 2 oz. stoned raisins to each lb. plums.
2 Simmer the raisins with the fruit.
3 When the jam has reached setting point, allow 2 oz. walnuts to each lb. of jam.

Mixed plum conserve

cooking time: approximately 25 minutes

you will need:

1 lb. cooking red plums (stoned)	no water if fruit is very ripe ($\frac{1}{4}$ pint if under-ripe)
1 lb. golden plums (stoned)	3 lb. sugar
1 lb. Victoria plums (stoned)	

1 Simmer red and golden plums until softened slightly with the water, if used.
2 Add halved or quartered Victoria plums and continue cooking until these are tender.
3 Add the sugar and stir until dissolved.
4 When dissolved boil rapidly until set.
This is a particularly delicious jam since you have the pieces of Victoria plum in a golden purée.

Plum cheeses

cooking time: 30 minutes

Use any of the recipes for plum jam (see before) and rub the fruit through a sieve. Allow 12 oz.–1 lb. sugar to each lb. or pint of purée. Stir until sugar has dissolved. Boil rapidly until set.

Victoria plum conserve

cooking time: 15 minutes

you will need:

1 lb. sugar	1 lb. Victoria plums
⅛ pint water	(stoned)

1 Boil the sugar and water together, stirring well, until the sugar has dissolved.
2 Put in the halved Victoria plums.
3 Cook steadily until the jam sets.
4 Add some of the kernels from the stones.

Prune jam

cooking time: 35 minutes

you will need:

1 lb. dried prunes	sugar
1 pint water	lemon juice

1 Soak prunes overnight in the water.
2 Simmer the prunes in this water until soft.
3 If necessary you can add a little extra water.
4 Remove the stones and measure the pulp.
5 Allow 1 lb. sugar and the juice of 1 lemon to each pint or lb. of pulp.
6 Stir until the sugar has dissolved.
7 Boil rapidly until set.

Prune conserve (1)

cooking time: 35 minutes

you will need:

1 lb. dried prunes*	1 lb. sugar
1 pint water	juice 2 lemons

*It is better to use rather small prunes in this preserve.

1 Soak the prunes overnight in the water.
2 Next day, lift out and drain, keeping the liquid.
3 Boil this prune liquid with the sugar and lemon juice, stirring well until the sugar has dissolved.
4 Add the prunes and simmer gently for approximately 25 minutes.

Prune conserve (2)

cooking time: 35 minutes

Use recipe and method for prune jam, but add 6 oz. chopped walnuts when this has reached setting point. The grated rind of 1 orange and lemon may be simmered with the prunes.

Pumpkin jam

cooking time: 40 minutes

you will need:

3 lb. pumpkin, peeled and diced	4 oz. crystallised ginger or 2 oz. root
grated rind and juice 2 lemons	ginger
	3 lb. sugar

1 Boil the pumpkin until it is tender.
2 Drain well and mash thoroughly.
3 Add the grated lemon rind and juice.
4 Add ginger cut into neat pieces. If dried ginger is used, this should be bruised, put in a muslin bag, cooked with the jam and removed before putting into jars.
5 Bring to the boil.
6 Add sugar and stir until dissolved.
7 Boil for 20 minutes or until thick.

Pumpkin and lemon jam

cooking time: 40 minutes

Use the recipe and method for pumpkin jam but use 3 lemons and omit the ginger.

Pumpkin and orange jam

cooking time: 40 minutes

Use the recipe and method for pumpkin jam but use 3 oranges and 1 lemon. The orange rind should be grated and the orange pulp added with the grated lemon and orange rind and lemon juice (point 3 in pumpkin jam).

Quince jam

cooking time: 35–45 minutes

you will need:

1 lb. quinces	1 lb. sugar
¼ pint water if fruit is ripe (1–⅛ pint if fruit is very firm)	juice ½ lemon

1 Peel, core and cut up the fruit*.
2 Simmer with the water until soft.
3 Add sugar and juice, stir until dissolved.
4 Boil rapidly until set.

*If desired the fruit could be grated instead of cut into pieces.

Quince and apple jam

cooking time: 35–45 minutes

you will need:

1 lb. quinces
1 lb. cooking apples (after peeling and coring)
⅛ pint water
2 lb. sugar

Use the method for quince jam.

Quince preserve

cooking time: 35–40 minutes

you will need:

1 lb. quinces
1 lb. sugar
½ pint water
juice 1 lemon

1 Peel and cut the quinces into neat pieces.
2 Simmer the sugar and water until the sugar has dissolved.
3 Put in the quinces with the lemon juice.
4 Cook slowly until the fruit is soft.

Quince cheeses

cooking time: 45 minutes

Use either of the recipes for quince jam and rub the fruit through a sieve. There is no need to peel or core the quinces if using this recipe.

1 Measure the pulp.
2 Allow 1 lb. sugar to each lb. or pint of purée.
3 Stir in the sugar.
4 Stir until dissolved over a steady heat.
5 Boil rapidly until set.

Raisin and cranberry jam

cooking time: 35 minutes

Add 3 oz. raisins to each lb. cranberries and proceed as for cranberry jam (see page 16).

Raspberry jam

cooking time: 8–10 minutes

you will need:

1 lb. raspberries
1 lb. sugar

1 Heat the fruit until boiling point is reached.
2 Stir in the hot sugar – heated for a few minutes in the oven.
3 Boil rapidly until the jam has set. If the fruit is firm and fresh, this should take only about 3 minutes of rapid boiling.

Raspberry and blackcurrant jam

cooking time: 25–30 minutes

you will need:

1 lb. blackcurrants
½ pint water
2 lb. raspberries
3 lb. sugar

1 Simmer the blackcurrants with the water until soft.
2 Add the raspberries and cook for a further few minutes.
3 Add sugar and stir until dissolved.
4 Boil rapidly until set.

Raspberry and redcurrant jam

cooking time: 10–15 minutes

you will need:

1 lb. redcurrants
⅛ pint water
1 lb. raspberries
2 lb. sugar

1 Heat the redcurrants with the water for about 5 minutes.
2 Add the raspberries and continue cooking until these are boiling.
3 Add sugar and stir until dissolved.
4 When dissolved boil rapidly until jam is set.

Raspberry and strawberry jam

cooking time: 10–12 minutes

1 lb. raspberries
1 lb. strawberries
juice 1 lemon
2 lb. sugar

Use method for raspberry jam.

Uncooked raspberry jam

you will need:

1 lb. sugar   1 lb. fresh
raspberries

1 Put the sugar to warm in a cool oven.
2 Mash the raspberries and stir in the warmed sugar.
3 Continue stirring until sugar has quite dissolved.
4 Put into pots and seal down.
This jam may not appear very stiff when first made, but the flavour is wonderful and it does stiffen with keeping.

Note
This recipe is suitable only for perfect fruit which is dry and freshly picked.

Rhubarb in jam making

The best flavoured rhubarb for jam is the second crop in the autumn. You can use spring rhubarb, but the flavour is not so good.

Rhubarb jam

cooking time: 25 minutes

you will need:

1 lb. rhubarb*   1 lb. sugar
*If rhubarb is very ripe you need the juice 1 lemon: if under-ripe lemon can be omitted.

1 Simmer the rhubarb with no water until soft. If the rhubarb is very hard, you may need 1 tablespoon water.
2 Stir in the sugar and lemon juice, and stir until sugar is dissolved.
3 Boil rapidly until set.

Rhubarb conserve

cooking time: 30 minutes

you will need:

2 lb. rhubarb   1 lemon
2 lb. sugar   1 orange
8 oz. stoned
  raisins

1 Cut up the rhubarb into 1½-inch pieces.

2 Cover with the sugar and leave to stand overnight.
3 Boil rhubarb, raisins and sugar gently for 20 minutes.
4 Add the juice and rind of the lemon and orange.
5 Boil until the syrup is thick and jelly-like but do not boil until jam forms a thick wrinkled surface.

Rhubarb preserve

cooking time: 25 minutes

Use recipe for rhubarb jam (see before), but sprinkle the sugar over the diced rhubarb, leave for several hours and then cook and stir steadily until sugar has dissolved. Add the lemon juice. Boil until syrup is thick.

Rhubarb and angelica jam

cooking time: 20 minutes

you will need:

1 lb. rhubarb   1 oz. angelica,
1 lb. sugar   chopped
juice 1 lemon

1 Cut rhubarb into pieces.
2 Cover with sugar and lemon juice and leave to stand overnight.
3 Add angelica.
4 Stir well.
5 Boil all together until set.

Rhubarb and dried fig jam

cooking time: 1 hour 20 minutes

you will need:

1 lb. dried figs   3 lb. sugar
1 pint water   juice 1 large lemon
2 lb. rhubarb, chopped

1 Soak the figs in the water for 48 hours, or even 72 hours.
2 Simmer until the figs are nearly soft.
3 Add the rhubarb.
4 Continue cooking until a thick pulp is formed.
5 Add the sugar and lemon juice, stir until dissolved.
6 Boil rapidly until set.

Rhubarb and ginger jam

cooking time: 25 minutes

you will need:

1 lb. rhubarb, chopped
1 teaspoon powdered
  ginger, or 1–2 oz.
  crystallised ginger

1 lb. sugar
juice 1 lemon

1 Use the recipe for either the rhubarb jam or rhubarb preserve.
2 The ginger should be chopped finely. If using powdered ginger it should be sprinkled over the rhubarb.

Strawberry jam

cooking time: 15 minutes

you will need:

1 lb. strawberries
  – good weight
14 oz. sugar

juice 1 lemon or $\frac{1}{8}$
  pint redcurrant juice

1 Simmer the fruit until soft.
2 Add the sugar and lemon juice and stir until sugar is dissolved.
3 Boil rapidly until set.

Strawberry jam (whole fruit)

cooking time: 12–15 minutes

Use ingredients as for strawberry jam, see above.
1 Pour sugar and fruit into pan.
2 Heat very gently until sugar has dissolved, stirring occasionally.
3 Add lemon or redcurrant juice.
4 Boil steadily until set.

Strawberry preserve

cooking time: 10–12 minutes

you will need:

1 lb. sugar
juice 1 lemon or
  $\frac{1}{4}$ pint redcurrant
  juice

1 lb. firm strawberries
  (medium sized)

1 Boil the sugar and lemon juice until the sugar has dissolved, stirring all the time.
2 Turn off the heat – leave the strawberries in the syrup for about 15 minutes.

3 Return to the heat and boil steadily for approximately 5–7 minutes.
4 The syrup does not set very firmly, but you have a wonderfully flavoured preserve.

Three fruit jam

cooking time: 20 minutes

you will need:

8 oz. raspberries
8 oz. redcurrants

8 oz. strawberries
1½ lb. sugar

Use method for raspberry jam (see page 27).

Red tomato jam

cooking time: 20 minutes

you will need:

2 lb. tomatoes
2 lb. sugar

4 tablespoons lemon
  juice

1 Cut the tomatoes into quarters.
2 Cover with sugar and stand overnight.
3 Simmer gently, stirring well until sugar has dissolved.
4 Continue simmering until tomatoes are soft.
5 Add lemon juice.
6 Boil rapidly until set.
7 You can alter the flavour by adding a little powdered or crystallised ginger.

Green tomato jam

cooking time: 30 minutes

Use recipe and method for red tomato jam. Green tomatoes are a good substitute for greengages.

Tomato preserve

cooking time: 15 minutes

you will need:

1 lb. sugar
$\frac{1}{4}$ pint water
1 teaspoon powdered
  ginger

1 lb. firm red tomatoes
juice 1 lemon

1 Boil sugar and water with the ginger until sugar has dissolved.
2 Cut tomatoes into quarters.
3 Put into the syrup, together with the lemon juice.
4 Cook steadily until soft.

Jellies

You will find some helpful hints on making jellies on page 8.

Many people think that jelly making is more complicated than making jam but the method is nearly the same. The preparation of the fruit takes less time than for jam, and this compensates for time taken to drain jelly.

Clarity depends on draining the pulp properly.

How to use a jelly bag

A proper jelly bag is made of heavy duty calico or flannel. It has a very close weave so that the juice only drains and none of the pulp comes through. This is important as even a small amount of pulp will give a cloudy jelly. Jelly bags are expensive to buy, but with care they will last for a very long time. If you cannot buy a jelly bag you could make one yourself if you buy flannel or calico.

Use a square 18–24 inches by 18–24 inches.

1 Form into a triangle and machine firmly down the seam, being particularly careful at the tip so that this is well joined.
2 Attach 4 pieces of tape to the top.

To hang a jelly bag
Tie the pieces of tape on the 4 'legs' of an up-turned chair with a bowl underneath so that the fruit can be put into the bag and allowed to drip through gently.

If you have no jelly bag
You can make do without a jelly bag, by using several thicknesses of fine muslin and hanging them from an upturned chair. You may also drain through muslin over a fine (not wire) sieve. But remember not to push it through, in any way, but allow it to drip in its own time.

Using the fruit twice in jelly
When using fruits such as cooking apples, red-currants, damsons, gooseberries, blackcurrants, all of which have a high setting quality, you can produce a greater yield of liquid by boiling the fruit twice.

Follow the recipe as given and when the juice has dripped through the jelly bag, return the pulp to the preserving pan. Put only half the first amount of water over the fruit, boil again. Strain, and mix with first amount of liquid.

Dissolving the sugar in jelly
By the time the juice has gone through the bag it will, of course, have become quite cold. Reheat this, but do not boil for any length of time before adding the sugar, then stir until the sugar has dissolved.

To fill pots with jelly
Fill jam jars while the jelly is still very hot, so it does not begin to set in the pan.

Apple jelly

cooking time: 25–30 minutes

you will need:

cooking apples or crab apples (unpeeled)	1 pint water to each 2 lb. fruit sugar

1 Simmer the fruit until a pulp; there is no need to either peel or core the fruit.
2 Put the pulp through thick muslin or a jelly bag.
3 Leave to strain overnight.
4 Measure the juice.
5 Allow 1 lb. sugar to each pint of juice.
6 Stir in the sugar.
7 Boil rapidly until set.

Apple and geranium jelly

cooking time: 25–30 minutes

Follow the recipe and method for apple jelly, but allow 2–3 fragrant geranium leaves to each lb. of apples.

Apple and lemon jelly

cooking time: 25–30 minutes

you will need:

2 lemons	½ pint water
1 lb. cooking apples (unpeeled)	sugar

1 Squeeze juice from lemons and pare off yellow part of rind.
2 Chop up apples, but do not peel or core.
3 Put apples, lemon rind and water into pan.
4 Simmer until soft.
5 Place the fruit in a jelly bag and leave to strain.
6 Add lemon juice.
7 Measure, and to each pint of liquid add 1 lb. sugar, stir until dissolved.
8 Boil rapidly until set.

Apple struper

cooking time: 45 minutes

you will need:

2 lb. cooking or crab apples (unpeeled)	honey (if liked) grated nutmeg mixed spice or cinnamon
1 pint water	
sugar	

1 Wash, but do not peel the apples.
2 Divide large ones into pieces keeping the core and pips as these help the jelly to set.
3 Simmer gently until a thick pulp.
4 Strain through a jelly bag.
5 Measure and allow to each pint of juice, 1 lb. sugar or ¾ lb. sugar and 4 oz. honey. These proportions will give the consistency of jelly.
6 If you wish, instead of putting the apple pulp through a jelly bag, the whole of the purée can be rubbed through a sieve so that you have more of a juice.

7 Allow to each pint of juice or purée, ½ level teaspoon grated nutmeg (up to 1 teaspoon could be used), and ¼ level teaspoon mixed spice or cinnamon.
8 Add spices when sugar is added and boil until setting point is reached.

Apple and orange jelly

cooking time: 25–30 minutes

Follow recipe and method for apple and lemon jelly, but use the grated rind of 2 oranges.

Blackberry or bramble jelly

cooking time: 25–30 minutes

you will need:

1 lb. blackberries	1 medium sized cooking apple*
¼ pint water	sugar

* Instead of using an apple you can use the juice of one lemon to each pound blackberries. Add this with sugar.

1 Put blackberries, water and apple into a pan.
2 Simmer until soft.
3 Strain the pulp through a jelly bag.
4 Measure juice and allow 1 lb. sugar to each pint.
5 Stir in sugar and continue stirring until dissolved.
5 Boil rapidly until set.

Spiced blackberry jelly

cooking time: 25–30 minutes

Use recipe and method for blackberry jelly but add 1 level teaspoon mixed spice to each pint juice. Stir in with the sugar.

Blackcurrant jelly

cooking time: 40 minutes

you will need:

2 lb. blackcurrants	sugar
1 pint water	

Use method for redcurrant jelly (see page 35).

Blackcurrant and redcurrant jelly

cooking time: 40 minutes

you will need:

1 lb. blackcurrants	1 pint water
1 lb. redcurrants	sugar

Use method for redcurrant jelly (see page 35).

Cranberry jelly

cooking time: 30 minutes

you will need:

2 lb. cranberries	sugar
¼ pint water	

1 Simmer cranberries with the water until soft.
2 Strain through jelly bag.
3 Allow 1 lb. sugar to each pint of juice.
4 Stir sugar until dissolved.
5 Boil rapidly until set.

Cranberry and grape jelly

cooking time: 30 minutes

you will need:

1 lb. cranberries	sugar
1 lb. white grapes	lemon juice
¼ pint water	

1 Simmer the cranberries and grapes in the water until soft.
2 Strain through jelly bag.
3 Allow 1 lb. sugar and juice of 1 lemon to each pint of juice.
4 Stir in sugar until dissolved.
5 Boil rapidly until set.

Cucumber jelly

cooking time: 30 minutes

you will need:

about 4 lb. cucumbers (unpeeled)	1 lemon
⅛ pint water	1 lb. sugar
	ginger

1 Cut up the cucumbers.
2 Add water and simmer until a soft pulp is formed.
3 Strain through a jelly bag.

4 Add the juice of 1 lemon, 1 lb. sugar and a pinch of ginger to each pint of juice.
5 Stir until the sugar has dissolved.
6 Boil rapidly until jelly sets.

Note

This is an extravagant jelly in that the cucumber yields little juice.

Damson jelly

cooking time: 30–35 minutes

you will need:

2 lb. damsons	sugar
¾ pint water if fruit is hard (¼ pint water if ripe)	

1 Simmer the fruit in the water until soft.
2 Strain through a jelly bag.
3 Measure the juice and allow 1 lb. sugar to each pint of juice.
4 Stir the sugar until sugar has dissolved.
5 Boil rapidly until set.

Damson and apple jelly

cooking time: 35 minutes

you will need:

1 lb. damsons	½ pint water if fruit is ripe (¾ pint water if firm)
1 lb. apples	
	sugar

1 Simmer fruit in the water until soft.
2 Put through jelly bag.
3 Allow 1 lb. sugar to each pint juice.
4 Stir the sugar until dissolved.
5 Boil rapidly until set.

Elderberry jelly

cooking time: 25 minutes

you will need:

4 lb. elderberries	sugar
1 pint water	1–2 lemons

1 Simmer the berries in the water.
2 When quite soft strain through a jelly bag.
3 To each pint juice add 12 oz. to 1 lb. sugar and the juice of a large lemon or 2 small lemons.
4 Stir well until sugar has dissolved.
5 Boil rapidly until setting point is reached.

Elderberry and apple jelly

cooking time: 30 minutes

you will need:

1 lb. cooking apples (unpeeled)	2 lb. elderberries
1 pint water	sugar
	juice 1 lemon

1 Cut up the apples, but do not peel or core.
2 Simmer for about 10 minutes till quite soft.
3 Add the elderberries and continue cooking until quite soft.
4 Strain through a jelly bag or muslin.
5 Measure the juice and to each pint add 1 lb. sugar and the juice of one lemon.
6 Stir well until sugar has dissolved.
7 Boil rapidly until set.

Gooseberry jelly

cooking time: 25 minutes

you will need:

1 lb. sharp green gooseberries	½ pint water
	sugar

1 Wash fruit and put into pan, with water – do not 'top and tail' fruit.
2 Simmer gently till fruit is very soft.
3 Put into jelly bag to drain.
4 Measure the juice, allowing 1 lb. sugar to each pint juice, stirring until sugar has dissolved.
5 Boil rapidly until set.

Gooseberry and redcurrant jelly

cooking time: 25 minutes

you will need:

1 lb. ripe gooseberries	½ pint water
1 lb. redcurrants	sugar

Use method for gooseberry jelly.

Greengage jelly

cooking time: 30 minutes

you will need:

2 lb. greengages	sugar
½ pint water if fruit is ripe (¾ pint if firm)	

Use method for Victoria plum jelly (see page 36).

Guava jelly

cooking time: 25–30 minutes

you will need:

2 lb. guava pulp	sugar
½ pint water	juice 2 lemons

1 Simmer the fruit with the water until very soft.
2 Put through a jelly bag.
3 Allow 1 lb. sugar to each pint juice.
4 Stir until dissolved. Add lemon juice.
5 Boil rapidly until set.

Leveller jelly

This is the name given to the very large dessert gooseberries and they make wonderful jelly.

cooking time: 25 minutes

you will need:

1 lb. fruit	sugar
¼ pint water	

Use method for gooseberry jelly.

Medlar jelly

cooking time: 30 minutes

you will need:

1 lb. medlars	½ level teaspoon citric or tartaric acid or juice ½ lemon
¼ pint water	
sugar	

1 Simmer fruit and water until soft.
2 Strain through a jelly bag.
3 Measure juice, allow 1 lb. sugar to each pint.
4 Stir in sugar and acid or lemon juice.
5 Continue stirring until dissolved.
6 Boil rapidly until set.

Medlar and lemon jelly

cooking time: 30 minutes

you will need:

1 lb. medlars	grated rind and juice 2 lemons
⅛ pint water	sugar

1 Simmer fruit, water and lemon rind until soft.
2 Strain through jelly bag and proceed as for medlar jelly.

Mint jelly (1)

cooking time: 5 minutes

you will need:

Syrup
8 oz. sugar
¼ pint water

¼ pint vinegar

1½ dessertspoons
  powdered gelatine
2–3 tablespoons mint,
  chopped

1 Make a syrup of the sugar and water, by boiling together.
2 Add the vinegar and the powdered gelatine.
3 Stir in chopped mint.
4 Pour into jars.
5 Seal down most thoroughly.
6 Store in a cool place.

Mint jelly (2)

cooking time: 30 minutes

you will need:

2 lb. sharp cooking
  apples (unpeeled)
or
2 lb. crab apples
  (unpeeled)

1 pint water
sugar
2 tablespoons
  vinegar
mint

1 To each pint of juice allow 1 lb. sugar and 2 tablespoons chopped mint.
2 Wash the apples and if large cut into pieces, but do NOT peel or core them.
3 Cover with water.
4 Simmer gently until they form a thick pulp.
5 Put through a jelly bag or since this may not be available, several thicknesses of muslin and leave dripping overnight.
6 Measure the juice and to each pint allow 1 lb. sugar.
7 Heat the juice and when boiling stir in the sugar.
8 Continue stirring until sugar has quite dissolved.
9 Boil rapidly until setting point is reached – without stirring.
10 Add the vinegar and the mint. If you are not very fond of the flavour of vinegar, it may be omitted.
11 The jelly will be a better colour if a few drops of green colouring are added.
12 Pour the jelly into jars.
13 Seal down as for jam.

Pineapple and mint jelly

cooking time: 15 minutes

you will need:

1 pint sweetened
  canned pineapple
  juice
juice 3 lemons

12 oz. sugar
1 tablespoon mint,
  chopped

1 Put the sweetened pineapple juice into a pan and bring to the boil.
2 Add lemon juice and sugar, stirring until sugar is dissolved.
3 Boil rapidly until set.
4 Stir in the chopped mint.

Mulberry jelly

cooking time: 45 minutes

you will need:

1 cooking apple
  (unpeeled)
1 lb. mulberries

¼ pint water
sugar

1 Cut up but do not peel or core the apple.
2 Simmer with the mulberries and water until soft.
3 Strain through a jelly bag.
4 Measure juice, allow 1 lb. sugar to each pint.
5 Stir together until sugar has dissolved.
6 Boil rapidly until set.

Quince jelly

cooking time: 50 minutes

you will need:

2 lb. quinces
2 pints water
  with ripe fruit

(use 3 pints for
  under-ripe fruit)
sugar

1 Do not peel or core the quinces, but just cut them up.
2 Simmer with the water until very soft.
3 Strain through a jelly bag and allow 1 lb. sugar to each pint juice.
4 Stir until dissolved.
5 Boil rapidly until set.

Note

If the quinces are very ripe, you can allow the juice of 1 lemon to each pint of juice to make certain it sets well.

Quince and apple jelly

cooking time: 50 minutes

you will need:

1 lb. apples
1 lb. quinces
sugar

1¼ pints water If fruit
is ripe (1½ if
under-ripe)

Use method for quince jelly. There is no need to use any lemon juice.

Rhubarb and strawberry jelly

cooking time: 20–30 minutes

you will need:

1 lb. strawberries
1 lb. rhubarb,
  sliced

2–3 tablespoons water
lemon
sugar

1 Simmer the strawberries and rhubarb in the water until very soft.
2 Strain through a jelly bag.
3 Measure the juice and allow the juice of 1 lemon and 1 lb. sugar to each pint of juice.
4 Stir in the sugar until dissolved.
5 Boil rapidly until set.

Raspberry jelly

cooking time: 20–25 minutes

you will need:

raspberries
¼ pint water to each
  1 lb. raspberries

sugar

1 Simmer fruit and water until soft.
2 Place in a jelly bag and leave to drain. Measure juice.
3 To each pint of juice add 1 lb. sugar, stir until sugar dissolves.
4 Boil rapidly until set.

Redcurrant jelly

cooking time: 25 minutes

you will need:

1 lb. redcurrants
¼ pint water

sugar

Use method for apple jelly (see page 30).

Redcurrant and loganberry jelly

cooking time: 20–25 minutes

you will need:

8 oz. redcurrants
8 oz. loganberries

½ pint water
sugar

1 Put fruit into pan with water.
2 Simmer gently until fruit is soft.
3 Put into a jelly bag and leave to drain.
4 Measure juice, allow 1 lb. sugar to each pint.
5 Heat and stir until sugar has dissolved.
6 Boil rapidly until set.

Rose hip jelly

cooking time: 50 minutes

you will need:

1 lb. rose hips
water
2 lb. apples

sugar
lemon juice

1 Simmer the rose hips with ½ pint water and apples with ½ pint water, separately.
2 Put both lots of fruit through separate jelly bags.
3 Mix together.
4 Allow 1 lb. sugar and the juice of 1 lemon to each pint.
5 Stir over low heat until sugar has dissolved.
6 Boil rapidly until jelly has set.

Rowanberry jelly

cooking time: 30 minutes

you will need:

4 lb. rowanberries
1 pint water

sugar
lemons

1 Simmer berries with the water.
2 When soft strain through a jelly bag.
3 To each pint of juice add 12 oz. of sugar (for sharp jelly), or 1 lb. sugar for a sweeter jelly. Add the juice of 1 large or 2 small lemons.
4 Stir well until sugar has dissolved.
5 Boil rapidly until setting point is reached.

Spiced jellies

Spiced jellies are excellent if a small amount of spice is added to the juice of the following. This makes them particularly suitable for serving with cold meats.

Spiced apple jelly – follow previous suggestion.

Spiced gooseberry jelly – follow previous suggestion.

Spiced cucumber jelly – follow previous suggestion.

Spiced rosehip jelly – follow previous suggestion.

Strawberry jelly

cooking time: 25 minutes

you will need:

1 lb. strawberries	2 tablespoons water
8 oz. redcurrants	sugar

1 Simmer the strawberries, redcurrants and water together.
2 Strain through a jelly bag.
3 Measure the juice and allow 1 lb. sugar to each pint of juice.
4 Stir until sugar dissolved, then boil rapidly until set.

If you have no redcurrants:
1 Simmer the strawberries by themselves.
2 To each pint of strawberry juice allow the juice of 2 lemons and 1 lb. sugar – put the lemon juice in with the sugar.

Strawberry and gooseberry jelly

cooking time: 25–30 minutes

you will need:

1 lb. gooseberries	sugar
¼ pint water	lemons
1 lb. strawberries	

1 Simmer the gooseberries with the water until nearly soft.
2 Add the strawberries.
3 Continue cooking until very soft.

4 Strain through a jelly bag.
5 To each pint add 1 lb. sugar and the juice of a lemon.
6 Boil rapidly until set, stirring until sugar has dissolved.

Red tomato jelly

cooking time: 30 minutes

you will need:

2 lb. ripe tomatoes	sugar
½ pint water	lemon

1 Halve the tomatoes and simmer with the water until a smooth pulp.
2 Strain through a jelly bag.
3 To each pint of juice allow 1 lb. sugar and juice of 1 lemon.
4 Stir until sugar has dissolved.
5 Boil rapidly until set.

Green tomato jelly

cooking time: 40 minutes

Use ingredients as for red tomato jelly, but allow double the amount of water.
This recipe can be flavoured with a little spice if wished.

Victoria plum jelly

cooking time: 30 minutes

you will need:

2 lb. Victoria plums	lemons
½ pint water	sugar

1 Simmer the plums in the water until soft.
2 Strain through a jelly bag.
3 To each pint allow the juice of 1 lemon and 1 lb. sugar.
4 Stir over heat until sugar is dissolved.
5 Boil rapidly until set.

Marmalades

Before making a marmalade, read through the directions for perfect jams, etc. see page 7, because the same rules apply.

There are, however, certain other points to remember:

1 In order to distribute the peel evenly in the marmalade, you must allow the preserve to cool slightly after cooking, then stir briskly, and pour into pots.
2 Times of cooking are given, but these may vary somewhat depending on the size of your pan, speed of cooking, etc.
3 To test if the peel is soft, take a piece between your finger and thumb. If you cannot rub the peel almost to nothing, you must continue cooking before adding the sugar. If you add the sugar in a marmalade before the peel is soft, you tend to toughen the peel and this will spoil the marmalade.
4 Although citrus fruits, such as lemons and bitter oranges, have a high degree of setting quality, this is very quickly passed, so do test your marmalades very carefully for setting (see page 7).
5 Although you must simmer the fruit for a long time to soften the peel, do not over-cook, otherwise you tend to spoil the colour (see page 8, point 18).
6 Remember the more of the white pith you put into the marmalade, the more bitter it will be, so if you do not like a bitter marmalade, remove some of this pith. However, since it has a high degree of setting quality, tie it with the pips in muslin.

To prepare fruit for marmalade

It is possible to prepare the fruit peel by putting it through a really good mincer. Or as many people prefer peel to be chunky it is preferable to shred it with a sharp knife. On an electric mincer, there is a special attachment that allows one to put the peel through the shredder.

Carrot marmalade

cooking time: 1½–2 hours

you will need:

3 lemons	1 pint water
2 lb. carrots	2 lb. sugar

1 Squeeze out the juice from the lemons.
2 Shred the peel as for a marmalade and soak for several hours or overnight.
3 Tie the pips in a muslin bag.
4 Cut the carrots into neat pieces and simmer with the lemons until tender.
5 Stir in the sugar and lemon juice, removing bag of pips.
6 Boil rapidly until set.

Carrot orange marmalade

cooking time: 1½–2 hours

Use recipe and method as before, but use 2 sweet oranges and 1 lemon instead of 3 lemons.

Clementine marmalade

cooking time: 1½–2 hours

Use the recipe and method for tangerine marmalade (see page 41) using clementines instead of tangerines.

Dark marmalade

cooking time: 1½–2 hours

1 Use recipe and method for Seville orange marmalade (1) (see page 40).
2 Boil oranges whole.
3 When adding the sugar, put in 1 good dessertspoon of black treacle* to each lb. of sugar.

*This gives a rich flavour and a dark colour.

Four fruit marmalade

cooking time: 2 hours

you will need:

1 Seville orange*	2 lemons*
1 grapefruit*	3½ pints water
1 sweet orange*	3½ lb. sugar

*all medium sized fruit.

1 Prepare fruit as for Seville orange marmalade (2) (see page 40).
2 Cook in the same way, adding fruit juice with the warmed sugar.
3 Continue as instructed in this recipe.

Ginger marmalade

cooking time: 30 minutes

you will need:

3 lb. sharp cooking apples (unpeeled)	sugar
1 pint water	8 oz. preserved ginger

1 Wash apples.
2 Slice – without peeling and coring.
3 Put into pan and simmer gently with the water until the fruit is well pulped.
4 Strain through jelly bag.
5 Weigh the juice.
6 Put into preserving pan with equal weight of sugar.
7 Add ginger, cut in pieces about ½ inch square.
8 Boil briskly for about 10 minutes.
9 Test for 'jelling' and if necessary continue to boil for a little longer.
10 Put into hot sterilised jars.
11 Cover with waxed circles and tie down immediately.

Grapefruit marmalade

cooking time: 1½–2 hours

you will need:

2 medium sized grapefruit	2¼ lb. sugar
2¼ pints water	juice 1 lemon

Use method for Seville orange marmalade (2) (see page 40).

Jelly marmalade

cooking time: 1½ hours

Note

Use the recipe for lemon marmalade (see page 39) or lime marmalade (see page 39), or orange marmalade (see page 39). While the ingredients are the same as these recipes the method is very different.

1 Shred half the peel from the oranges very finely indeed.
2 The other half of the peel need not be shredded but tied in a bag of muslin.
3 The pips, pith and pulp of the fruit should also be tied in another bag of muslin.
4 Put the shredded peel and the 2 bags to soak overnight, in the water.
5 Simmer gently the next day for about 1 hour.
6 Take out the 2 bags and discard.
7 Add sugar and lemon juice. Stir over low heat till sugar is dissolved.
8 Bring to the boil and boil until set.

Note

If, by chance, you do not want any peel in the marmalade at all, as would be the case with someone suffering from an ulcer, then all the peel is tied in a bag.

Apricot and lemon marmalade

cooking time: 1½ hours

you will need:

1 lb. lemons	3 pints water
1 lb. dried apricots	3 lb. sugar

1 Prepare the lemons as for orange marmalade (2) (see page 41) tying the pips in a muslin bag and squeezing out the juice.
2 Soak overnight, together with the apricots, in the water.
3 Simmer next day until soft, removing pips.
4 Stir in lemon juice and sugar, stirring until sugar has dissolved.
5 Boil rapidly until set.

Lemon marmalade

cooking time: 1½–2 hours

you will need:

1 lb. lemons (4 medium or 3 large lemons)	2½ pints water 2½ lb. sugar

Use method for orange marmalade (2) (see page 41).

Lime marmalade

cooking time: 1½–2 hours

you will need:

1 lb. limes 2½ pints water	2½ lb. sugar

1 Cut or mince the limes finely, removing pips.
2 Soak the peel and pulp overnight in the water, together with the pips, which should be tied up carefully in a piece of muslin.
3 After soaking put the fruit, water and pips in a covered pan.
4 Simmer slowly for approximately 1½ hours. until peel is quite soft.
5 Take out the bag of pips.
6 Stir in the warmed sugar, until sugar is dissolved.
7 Bring the marmalade to the boil.
8 Boil rapidly in an uncovered pan until set – approximately 20 minutes.

Mint marmalade

cooking time: 1½–2 hours

Use recipe and method for lemon marmalade, and when setting point is reached, add 1 tablespoon chopped fresh mint to each lb. marmalade.

Orange and lemon marmalade

cooking time: 1½–2 hours

you will need:

1 lb. sweet oranges 3½ lb. sugar	1 lb. lemons 3½ pints water

Use method for Seville orange marmalade (2) (see page 40).

Quince marmalade

cooking time: 45 minutes

you will need:

1 lb. quinces ½ pint water	1¼ lb. sugar juice 1 lemon

1 Peel, core and cut the quinces into fairly even slices.
2 Put into the water.
3 Simmer gently until tender. If the quinces are very hard you may find you need a little more water.
4 Add the sugar and lemon and stir until sugar has dissolved.
5 Boil until set.

Orange peel marmalade

cooking time: 1½–2 hours

you will need:

5 oz. orange peel juice 3 lemons	2 pints water 2 lb. sugar

Use method for Seville orange marmalade (2) (see page 40).
This is a very economical way of making marmalade, since it allows you to eat the fruit of the sweet oranges.

Orange peel and apple marmalade

cooking time: 1½–2 hours depending on thickness of peel

you will need:

peel from 1 lb. oranges 3 pints water	1 lb. cooking apples (peeled and cored) 3 lb. sugar

1 Soak the peel overnight in the water.
2 Simmer until nearly soft.
3 Add the apples.
4 Continue cooking until fruit forms a smooth pulp.
5 Stir in the sugar.
6 Boil without stirring until setting point is reached.

Rhubarb marmalade

cooking time: 1½ hours

you will need:

3 lemons	3 lb. rhubarb, diced
1½ pints water	3½ lb. sugar

1 Prepare the lemons as in method for orange marmalade (2) (see page 41) and soak overnight in the water, with the pips tied in a piece of muslin.
2 Simmer gently until the peel is nearly soft.
3 Add the diced rhubarb and continue cooking until tender.
4 Remove bag of pips.
5 Stir in the sugar and lemon juice, stirring until sugar has dissolved.
6 Boil rapidly until set.

Seville or bitter orange marmalade (1) (coarse cut and bitter)

cooking time: 2 hours

you will need:

1 lb. Seville or bitter oranges (3 medium sized oranges)	2 pints water 2 lb. sugar

1 Wash oranges thoroughly.
2 Put whole oranges into covered pan with the water.
3 Simmer slowly for about 1½ hours or until a blunt wooden skewer will easily pierce the skin.
4 Remove oranges from liquid.
5 Allow to cool.
6 Cut up neatly.
7 Put pips into liquid and boil steadily for 10 minutes to extract the pectin from them.
8 Remove pips with a perforated spoon, and replace the cut orange pulp.
9 Bring to the boil.
10 Stir in the warmed sugar.
11 Continue stirring until sugar is dissolved.
12 Bring to the boil and boil rapidly without stirring until setting point is reached. It is advisable to start testing the marmalade after about 15 minutes.

Seville or bitter orange marmalade (2) (a sweeter variety)

cooking time: 1½–2 hours

you will need:

1 lb. Seville or bitter oranges	juice lemon or 1 level teaspoon citric or tartaric acid
3 pints water	
3 lb. sugar	

1 Cut or mince oranges finely, removing pips.
2 Soak peel and pulp overnight in the water, together with the pips tied up in a piece of muslin.
3 After soaking, put fruit, water and pips into a covered pan.
4 Simmer slowly until peel is quite soft. This should take about 1½ hours, but the cooking time will vary with thickness of peel.
5 Take out the bag of pips.
6 Stir in warmed sugar and lemon juice or acid.
7 Bring marmalade to the boil.
8 Boil rapidly in an uncovered pan until setting point is reached. This will take about 20 minutes. Start testing with small quantities after 10 minutes.

Scotch marmalade

cooking time: 1¾ hours

you will need:

2 sweet oranges	water
2 lemons	sugar
1 grapefruit **or** 2 bitter or Seville oranges	

1 Wipe fruit with a damp cloth.
2 Quarter, and cut through again.
3 Slice finely with a sharp knife, removing the pips which place in a small basin.
4 To each pound of cut fruit add 3 pints water.
5 Cover pips with some of the water.
6 Set aside for 24 hours.
7 Boil the cut fruit until soft (about 1–1¼ hours), adding the juice from the pips before boiling.
8 Put aside until cool enough to weigh.
9 To every pound of boiled fruit allow 1¼ lb. sugar and stir until sugar has dissolved.

10 Boil until it jellies. A period of 15 minutes fast boiling should be enough.

Variation
Using less sugar—allow only 1 lb. sugar to each lb. of boiled fruit if you prefer more 'bite'.

Sweet orange marmalade (1)

cooking time: 1¼–1½ hours

you will need:

1 lb. sweet oranges	2 lb. sugar
2 pints water	juice 1 lemon

Use method for Seville orange marmalade (1) (see page 40) adding lemon juice at step 10. The peel tends to soften more quickly with Seville oranges.

Sweet orange marmalade (2)

cooking time: 1½–2 hours

you will need:

1 lb. sweet oranges	2 lb. sugar
2 pints water	juice 2 lemons

Use method for Seville orange marmalade (2) (see page 40).

Seville or bitter orange and tangerine marmalade

cooking time: 1½–2 hours

you will need:

6 bitter oranges	3 tangerines
1 lemon	6 pints water
3 lb. sugar	

Proceed as for Seville orange marmalade (2) (see page 40).

Tangerine marmalade

cooking time: 1½–2 hours

you will need:

1 lb. tangerines (5 medium-sized tangerines)	1½ lb. sugar 1 level teaspoon citric or tartaric acid or lemon juice
1½ pints water	

1 Cut the tangerines finely, removing the pips.

2 Soak the peel and pulp overnight in the water, together with the pips, which should be tied up carefully in a piece of muslin.
3 After soaking, put the fruit, water and pips into a covered pan.
4 Simmer slowly for approximately 1½ hours, until the peel is quite soft.
5 Take out the bag of pips.
6 Stir in the warmed sugar and lemon juice or acid, and stir till sugar is dissolved.
7 Bring the marmalade to the boil.
8 Boil rapidly in an uncovered pan until setting point is reached. This will take approximately 20 minutes.

Three fruit marmalade

cooking time: 1½–2 hours

you will need:

1 Seville orange or grapefruit*	1 lemon*
1 sweet orange*	2¼ pints water 2¼ lb. sugar

*all medium sized fruit.

1 Prepare the fruit as for orange marmalade (2) (see page 41).
2 Cook in the same way, adding the fruit juice with the warmed sugar.
3 Continue as instructed in recipe for orange marmalade.

Tomato marmalade

cooking time: 1½ hours

you will need:

3 lemons	3 lb. green tomatoes
1½ pints water	3½ lb. sugar

1 Prepare lemons as for orange marmalade (2) (see page 40) and soak overnight in the water, tying the pips in a piece of muslin.
2 Simmer gently until the peel is nearly soft.
3 Add the quartered tomatoes and continue cooking until these are tender but unbroken.
4 Remove bag of pips.
5 Stir in the sugar and lemon juice, stirring until sugar has dissolved.
6 Boil rapidly until set.

Using jams and jellies in cooking

Jam glaze for cakes

This is enough to cover a 6–7 inch sponge or 12 small cakes and makes a change from icing.

you will need:

6 tablespoons sieved jam*	3 tablespoons water
1 teaspoon arrowroot	½ tablespoon lemon juice

*Any jam may be used for this but apricot or raspberry are particularly good.

1 Put the jam into the saucepan.
2 Blend the arrowroot with the water and lemon juice.
3 Boil together, stirring from time to time, until clear.
4 Cool slightly then spread over the cake or cakes.

Redcurrant glaze

This can be used for a thin coating on cakes but its chief purpose is to coat the fruit in flans, etc.

you will need:

3–4 level tablespoons redcurrant jelly	1 level teaspoon arrowroot of cornflour
	¼ pint syrup*

*from the cooked, canned or frozen fruit.

1 Put the jelly into the saucepan.
2 Blend the arrowroot or cornflour with the syrup, put into the pan with the jelly.
3 Boil steadily, stirring from time to time, until clear.
4 Cool, but do not allow this to become too stiff, then brush or spread over the fruit in the flan.

Variation

Apricot glaze – follow the recipe for Redcurrant glaze, but use sieved apricot jam instead.

Jam sauce

you will need:

4–6 tablespoons jam	8 tablespoons water
1 teaspoon arrowroot or cornflour	

1 Sieve the jam if wished, put into a saucepan.
2 Blend the arrowroot or cornflour with the water, add to the jam.
3 Boil steadily, stirring from time to time, until clear.
4 Serve hot with steamed puddings or cold with blancmange or ice cream.

Variations

Apricot ginger sauce – follow the recipe for Jam sauce, using apricot jam and 1 tablespoon syrup from preserved ginger in place of 1 tablespoon of the water. When thickened add 2 tablespoons thinly sliced preserved ginger.
Delicious hot or cold on ice cream.
Berry sauce – follow recipe for Jam sauce, but use a mixture of redcurrant jelly, raspberry and strawberry jams.
Coconut jam sauce – make the Jam sauce, then add 2 tablespoons desiccated coconut just before serving.
Chocolate apricot sauce – follow the recipe for Jam sauce using apricot jam. Blend 1 *level* tablespoon cocoa with the arrowroot or corn-flour and water and add.
Delicious on steamed chocolate pudding.
Coffee apricot sauce – follow the recipe for Jam sauce using apricot jam. Blend the arrowroot or cornflour with fairly weak coffee instead of water and add.
Delicious on steamed chocolate or coffee puddings.
Lemon marmalade sauce – follow the recipe for Jam sauce, but use lemon marmalade instead of jam and 6 tablespoons water and 2 tablespoons lemon juice instead of all water.
Other marmalade can be used instead.

Marshmallow jam sauce – make the Jam sauce, add about 8 halved marshmallows to the hot sauce.

Serve over ice cream while sauce is warm.

Mock Melba sauce – recipe as Jam sauce but use 3 tablespoons raspberry jam and 3 tablespoons redcurrant jelly and 5 tablespoons water only.

Spiced jam sauce – Jam sauce, page 42, is delicious if ½–1 teaspoon mixed spice is added just before serving.

Tutti fruitti sauce – follow the recipe for Jam sauce.

When the sauce has *just* thickened add:

1 tablespoon blanched almonds
1 tablespoon halved glacé cherries
1 tablespoon sultanas.

Jam filling

To fill 6–7 inch sponge

you will need:

1 oz. butter	4 tablespoons fine
1 oz. sugar	sweet biscuit or
1 tablespoon water	sponge cake crumbs
4 tablespoons jam	

1 Heat the butter, sugar and water in a pan.
2 Add the jam and heat very gently.
3 Stir the crumbs into the hot mixture and blend thoroughly.
4 Cool before using as a filling.

Variations

Apple ginger filling – follow the recipe for Jam filling but use crushed ginger-nut biscuits and apple jam or apple jelly. A tablespoon diced preserved ginger may be added, if wished, with the crumbs.

Lemon crumb filling – use lemon curd in place of jam in the Jam filling; omit sugar if wished.

Macaroon filling – follow recipe for Jam filling but use macaroon crumbs and apricot jam.

Orange filling – follow recipe for Jam filling but use 1 tablespoon orange juice in place of water plus finely grated rind of an orange and 4 tablespoons marmalade.

Jelly frosting

This is enough for the top of a 6–7 inch cake.

you will need:

2 level tablespoons redcurrant or other jelly	1 egg white

1 Put the jelly into a pan and warm until melted then cool slightly.
2 Whisk the egg white until very stiff.
3 Gradually whisk in the melted jelly then pile on the cake.

This remains quite firm and is very like marshmallow in texture.

Sieved jam or marmalade could be used instead of jelly.

Variation

Lemon frosting – follow the recipe for Jelly frosting but use 1½ tablespoons warmed lemon curd in place of jelly. Add ¼ teaspoon finely grated lemon rind to the curd for extra flavour.

Jam and jelly icing

Blend icing sugar with a smooth jam or jelly instead of water to coat cakes; the following are particularly suitable. You need about 2 tablespoons jam to each 8 oz. icing sugar. The jam or jelly should be warmed so you can mix the ingredients easily. Remember you never have a completely firm set icing, but a rather soft one.

Try:

Sieved apricot jam to coat the top of gingerbreads.

Apple jelly for gingerbreads or plain sponges.

Raspberry jam for sponges – top with chopped nuts or desiccated coconut.

Coconut almond topping

3 tablespoons sieved apricot jam	2 tablespoons finely chopped almonds
3 tablespoons desiccated coconut	

Blend 3 good tablespoons sieved apricot jam, desiccated coconut and finely chopped almonds. Spread over a plain cake and brown lightly under a low grill.

Variation

Coconut raspberry topping – use recipe for Coconut almond topping but substitute raspberry jam for apricot and chopped walnuts for almonds.

Jam in cooking

Jam may be used as a flavouring and sweetening ingredient in cakes and puddings. Never use more than half jam and half sugar and reduce the amount of liquid slightly, e.g.

In a gingerbread – instead of 4 oz. sugar use 2 oz. sugar and 2 oz. apricot jam or jelly marmalade.

In a family fruit cake – instead of 4 oz. sugar use 2 oz. sugar and 2 oz. bitter marmalade.

In a sponge pudding – instead of 4 oz. sugar use 2 oz. sugar and 2 oz. apricot, raspberry or other jam.

To flavour a sweet white or custard sauce
With lemon curd, jam, jelly or marmalade; reduce or omit the sugar. Stir about 2–3 tablespoonfuls into the sauce when thickened.

Jams and jellies in savoury dishes

(a) Add a little jam to a curry sauce; plum jam is particularly good.
(b) Stir a little redcurrant or apple jelly into the gravy of game or other casseroles or stews.

Jams, jellies and marmalades using commercial pectin

The object of using commercial pectin in jams is to give an easy set and this is particularly useful in the case of fruits that have little natural setting quality. Also by using commercial pectin it is possible to make a good jam, jelly or marmalade without being too extravagant with fruit.

The jars are filled and covered in the same way as for ordinary jams.

Apple and apricot jam

cooking time: 30 minutes

you will need:

1¾ lb. canned apricots	3¼ lb. sugar
12 oz. cooking apples (after peeling)	1 lemon
	1 bottle commercial pectin

1 Drain syrup from canned apricots.
2 Core and slice apples.
3 Cook until tender in ¼ pint of syrup from the apricots.
4 Turn apples into preserving pan.
5 Add apricots, sugar and lemon juice.

6 Heat gently, stirring occasionally, until sugar has dissolved.
7 Bring quickly to a full rolling boil.
8 Boil hard for 2 minutes.
9 Remove from heat and stir in commercial pectin.
10 Stir and skim by turns for 5 minutes to prevent the fruit from rising.
11 Pot and cover in the usual way.

Apricot and pineapple jam (canned fruit)

cooking time: 15 minutes

you will need:

1¼ lb. canned pineapple	2¾ lb. sugar
1¼ lb. canned apricots (or a mixture of these fruits to make 2¼ lb.)	1 lemon
	1 bottle commercial pectin

1 Chop the pineapple finely.
2 Put into preserving pan with apricots, sugar and lemon juice.
3 Heat gently, stirring occasionally, until sugar has dissolved.
4 Bring quickly to a full rolling boil.
5 Boil hard for 2 minutes.
6 Remove from heat and stir in the pectin.
7 Stir and skim by turns for 5 minutes to prevent fruit rising.
8 Pot and cover in the usual way.

Banana and pineapple jam

cooking time: 15 minutes

you will need:

5 ripe bananas	3¼ lb. sugar
1 20-oz. can crushed or chopped pineapple	1 bottle commercial pectin

1 Peel the bananas and mash thoroughly.
2 Put into a preserving pan with the crushed or chopped pineapple and sugar.

3 Heat gently, stirring occasionally until the sugar has dissolved.
4 Bring quickly to the boil.
5 Boil hard for 1 minute, and continue as previous recipe.

Dried apricot jam

cooking time: 40 minutes

you will need:

8 oz. dried apricots	3 lb. sugar
1½ pints water	1 bottle commercial pectin
3 tablespoons lemon juice (1 lemon)	

1 Wash fruit.
2 Leave to soak for at least 4 hours in the 1½ pints water.
3 Cover and simmer for about 30 minutes to break up the fruit.
4 Measure 1½ pints prepared fruit pulp, making up the amount with water if necessary.
5 Add lemon juice and sugar.
6 Heat slowly, stirring occasionally until the sugar has dissolved.
7 Bring to a full rolling boil and boil rapidly for 1 minute and continue as Apricot and pineapple jam.

Blackcurrant and pineapple jam (canned fruit)

cooking time: 20 minutes

you will need:

1 orange	2 lb. sugar
1 16-oz. can pineapple titbits or chunks	½ bottle commercial pectin
3 16-oz. cans blackcurrants	

1 Wash orange and grate rind.
2 Crush pineapple titbits or chunks.
3 Put blackcurrants, crushed pineapple, juice and orange rind into a saucepan with sugar. Do not use fruit syrup from cans.
4 Heat slowly, stirring occasionally, until sugar is dissolved.
5 Bring to a full rolling boil.
6 Boil rapidly for 2 minutes, and continue as previous recipe.

Cherry jam

cooking time: 25 minutes

you will need:

2½ lb. morello
  cherries (stoned)
¼ pint water
3 tablespoons lemon
  juice (1 lemon)

3 lb. sugar
1 bottle commercial
  pectin

1 Simmer the cherries in the water and lemon juice in a covered pan for about 15 minutes.
2 Add the sugar.
3 Heat slowly, stirring occasionally, until sugar has dissolved.
4 Bring to a full rolling boil.
5 Boil rapidly for 3 minutes.
6 Stir in commercial pectin.
7 Continue boiling for 1 minute.
8 Remove from heat and skim if necessary.
9 Cool slightly.
10 Pot and cover in the usual way.

Variation

With almond essence – for cherry jam with a stronger flavour add ¼ teaspoon almond essence before potting.

Black cherry jam

cooking time: 25 minutes

you will need:

2½ lb. black
  cherries (stoned)
¼ pint water
juice 2 lemons

3 lb. sugar
1 bottle commercial
  pectin

1 Put prepared fruit in pan with water and lemon juice.
2 Cook gently with lid on for 15 minutes.
3 Remove the lid and add sugar.
4 Stir over low heat until dissolved.
5 Bring to rolling boil.
6 Boil rapidly for 3 minutes.
7 Remove from heat.
8 Add pectin and stir well.
9 Cool for 15 minutes, stirring occasionally to prevent fruit rising.
10 Pot and cover in the usual way.

Gooseberry jam

cooking time: 25 minutes

you will need:

4 lb. gooseberries
½ pint water
6½ lb. sugar

1 bottle commercial
  pectin

1 Put gooseberries in a large saucepan or preserving pan with the water.
2 Bring to the boil.
3 Simmer, covered, for 15 minutes, or until the skins are soft, stirring occasionally.
4 Add sugar.
5 Heat slowly until sugar is dissolved, stirring occasionally.
6 Bring to a full rolling boil quickly.
7 Boil rapidly for 2 minutes, stirring occasionally.
8 Remove from heat and stir in commercial pectin.
9 Skim if necessary.
10 Allow to cool slightly.
11 Pot and cover in the usual way.
   When making half the quantity the fruit and sugar need to be boiled for 1 minute only.

Plum jam

cooking time: 28–30 minutes

you will need:

5 lb. plums
  (whole)
½ pint water
juice 1 lemon (if fruit
  is sweet)

6½ lb. sugar
¼ bottle commercial
  pectin

1 Wash the plums and cut into pieces, removing as many of the stones as desired.
2 Put the fruit and water into a large pan.
3 Add lemon juice if used.
4 Bring to the boil.
5 Cover and simmer for 15 minutes, stirring occasionally.
6 Add sugar.
7 Heat slowly until the sugar has dissolved, stirring occasionally.
8 Bring to a full rolling boil.
9 Boil rapidly for 3 minutes, stirring occasionally.
10 Remove from heat and stir in commercial pectin.

11 Skim if necessary.
12 Allow to cool to prevent fruit floating.
13 Pot and cover in the usual way.

Raspberry jam

cooking time: 12–15 minutes

you will need:

4 lb. raspberries
5½ lb. sugar

1 bottle commercial
pectin

1 Crush the berries.
2 Add the sugar.
3 Heat slowly until sugar has dissolved, stirring occasionally.
4 Bring to a full rolling boil quickly.
5 Boil rapidly for 2 minutes, stirring occasionally.
6 Remove from heat.
7 Stir in pectin.
8 Skim if necessary.
9 Pot and cover in the usual way.

Rhubarb jam

cooking time: 15–20 minutes

you will need:

2 lb. rhubarb
¼ pint water
3 tablespoons
lemon juice
½ oz. bruised root
ginger

2 oz. crystallised
ginger
3 lb. sugar
½ bottle commercial
pectin

1 Chop rhubarb very finely.
2 Place in preserving pan with the water.
3 Add lemon juice and the bruised root ginger in a muslin bag.
4 Bring to the boil and simmer gently for a few minutes until rhubarb is tender.
5 Add chopped crystallised ginger and sugar.
6 Heat slowly until sugar has dissolved.
7 Bring to full rolling boil quickly.
8 Boil rapidly for 3 minutes.
9 Remove from heat and take out muslin bag.
10 Stir in commercial pectin.
11 Allow to cool slightly to prevent fruit floating.
12 Pot and cover in the usual way.

Strawberry jam

cooking time: 15–20 minutes

you will need:

2¼ lb. small
strawberries
3 tablespoons lemon
juice

3 lb. sugar
knob butter or
margarine
½ bottle commercial
pectin

1 Put fruit in pan with lemon juice and sugar.
2 Stand for 1 hour, stirring occasionally.
3 Place over low heat, stirring occasionally.
4 When sugar has dissolved, add small knob of butter or margarine to reduce foaming.
5 Bring to full rolling boil.
6 Boil rapidly for 4 minutes, stirring occasionally.
7 Remove from heat.
8 Add commercial pectin and stir well.
9 Cool for at least 20 minutes to prevent fruit floating.
10 Pot and cover in the usual way.

Gooseberry jelly

cooking time: 30 minutes

you will need:

3 lb. gooseberries
1½ pints water
3¼ lb. sugar

½ bottle commercial
pectin
green colouring

1 Wash the gooseberries (there is no need to top and tail them).
2 Put them in a pan with the water.
3 Simmer, covered, for 20 minutes, or until the fruit is soft enough to mash.
4 Strain through a jelly bag.
5 Measure the juice into a pan and if necessary add water to make up to 2 pints.
6 Add the sugar.
7 Heat gently, stirring occasionally, until sugar has dissolved.
8 Stir in commercial pectin.
9 Bring to a full rolling boil.
10 Continue boiling for 1 minute.
11 Remove from heat.
12 Skim and stir in colouring if desired.
13 Pot and cover in the usual way.

Grape jelly

cooking time: 18–20 minutes

you will need:

3 lb. ripe black grapes	3 tablespoons lemon juice
¼ pint water	1 bottle commercial pectin
3¼ lb. sugar	

1 Use only fully ripe grapes.
2 Crush fruit thoroughly and put in a saucepan with the water.
3 Bring to the boil.
4 Simmer, covered, for 10 minutes.
5 Place the fruit in a jelly bag and leave to drain.
6 Measure the sugar, lemon juice and 1¼ pints grape juice into a large saucepan.
7 Heat slowly until the sugar has dissolved, stirring occasionally.
8 Bring to the boil and stir in commercial pectin.
9 Bring to a full rolling boil and boil rapidly for ½ minute.
10 Remove from the heat.
11 Skim.
12 Cool, pot and cover in the usual way.

Orange jelly

cooking time: 20–25 minutes

you will need:

6 oranges*	2 lb. 10 oz. sugar
1 large lemon*	1 bottle commercial pectin
water	

*approximately ¾ pint fruit juice.

1 Wash the oranges and the lemon.
2 Cut in halves and extract all the juice.
3 Cover the orange peel with water.
4 Bring to the boil.
5 Cover and simmer for 10 minutes.
6 Strain the liquid.
7 Add sufficient to the fruit juices to make 1 pint in all.
8 Place in a heavy saucepan with the sugar.
9 Stir over a low heat until the sugar has dissolved.
10 Bring to full rolling boil and boil rapidly for 2 minutes.
11 Remove from heat and stir in commercial pectin.

12 Bring back to boil and boil for 30 seconds.
13 Skim if necessary.
14 Allow to cool.
15 Pot and cover in the usual way.

Quince jelly

cooking time: 1¼ hours

you will need:

2 lb. quinces	½ bottle commercial pectin
2½ pints water	
sugar	

1 Cut up the fruit.
2 Simmer in the water for about 1 hour in a covered pan until tender.
3 Strain through a jelly bag.
4 Measure the juice and add 1 lb. of sugar to each pint.
5 Heat slowly, stirring occasionally, until the sugar has dissolved.
6 Add commercial pectin and boil rapidly for 1 minute.
7 Remove from heat and skim if necessary.
8 Pot and cover in the usual way.

Pineapple jelly

cooking time: 10 minutes

you will need:

1 20-oz. can pineapple juice	1 teaspoon lemon juice
2½ lb. sugar	1 bottle commercial pectin

1 Put the pineapple juice, sugar and lemon juice into a saucepan.
2 Heat gently, stirring occasionally, until the sugar has dissolved.
3 Bring quickly to a full rolling boil.
4 Stir in the pectin.
5 Boil hard for ½ minute.
6 Skim.
7 Pot and cover in the usual way.

Strawberry jelly

cooking time: 25–27 minutes

you will need:

3 lb. strawberries	3 tablespoons lemon
$\frac{3}{4}$ pint water	juice
$3\frac{1}{4}$ lb. sugar	1 bottle commercial
	pectin

1 Put the strawberries into a saucepan and crush thoroughly.
2 Add the water.
3 Bring to the boil.
4 Cover and simmer for 15 minutes.
5 Place in a cloth and allow the juice to drain.
6 Measure the juice and if necessary add the water to make up to 2 pints.
7 Put the juice, sugar and lemon juice into a preserving pan.
8 Heat gently, stirring occasionally, until the sugar has dissolved.
9 Bring quickly to a full rolling boil.
10 Boil hard for 2 minutes.
11 Remove from the heat and stir in commercial pectin.
12 Boil rapidly for a further minute.
13 Remove from heat.
14 Skim if necessary.
15 Pot and cover in the usual way.

Dried apricot and orange marmalade

cooking time: 1–$1\frac{1}{4}$ hours

you will need:

4 oz. dried apricots	$2\frac{1}{2}$ lb. sugar
$1\frac{1}{2}$ pints water	knob of butter
2 Seville oranges	$\frac{1}{2}$ bottle commercial
or 3 sweet oranges	pectin
1 lemon	
$\frac{1}{4}$ level teaspoon	
bicarbonate of soda	

1 Soak the apricots overnight in $\frac{1}{2}$ pint of the water.
2 Peel the rind from the oranges and lemon, being careful not to include any pith.
3 Remove the pith from the fruit also.
4 Shred the peel, and simmer it in the remaining pint of water with the bicarbonate of soda.
5 Slice the oranges and lemon and discard the pips.
6 Add the pulp, juice, apricots and 'soaking' water.
7 Boil for 20 minutes.
8 Add sugar and knob of butter.
9 Stir over a gentle heat until sugar is dissolved.
10 Boil for 5 minutes as fast as possible.
11 Remove from heat.
12 Stir in commercial pectin.
13 Skim if necessary.
14 Pot and cover in the usual way.

Orange ginger marmalade

cooking time: $1\frac{1}{4}$–$1\frac{1}{2}$ hours

you will need:

3 lb. oranges	4 oz. crystallised
2 lemons	ginger
$1\frac{1}{2}$ pints water	knob of butter
1 level teaspoon	1 bottle commercial
bicarbonate of soda	pectin
$4\frac{3}{4}$ lb. sugar	

1 Remove skins in quarters using a sharp knife.
2 Shave off and discard about half of white part (pith).
3 Shred skins very finely.
4 Place in preserving pan with water and soda (this helps to soften skins).
5 Bring to the boil.
6 Simmer, covered, for about 30–40 minutes stirring occasionally, until the skins can be crushed easily between thumb and forefinger.
7 Cut up the peeled fruit, discarding the pips and tough skin.
8 Add pulp and juice to cooked rind.
9 Cover and simmer for 20 minutes longer.
10 Put sugar, chopped ginger and 3 pints of prepared fruit into a large preserving pan, making up the quantity with water if necessary.
11 Heat slowly, stirring occasionally, until the sugar has dissolved.
12 Add a small piece of butter or margarine.
13 Bring to a full rolling boil.
14 Boil for 5 minutes.
15 Remove preserving pan from heat and stir in commercial pectin.
16 Stir and skim in turns for just 7 minutes to cool slightly and to prevent fruit floating.
17 Pour into clean hot jars and cover in the usual way.

Orange and grapefruit marmalade

cooking time: 1¼–1½ hours

you will need:

3 lb. citrus fruit (4
  oranges, 2 grapefruit
  and 1 lemon)
1½ pints water
1 level teaspoon
  bicarbonate of soda

5 lb. sugar
knob of butter
1 bottle commercial
  pectin

1 Wash fruit.
2 Remove skins by cutting in quarters using sharp knife.
3 Shave off and discard about half of white part (pith).
4 Shred skins very finely.
5 Place in preserving pan with water and soda (this helps to soften the skins).
6 Bring to the boil.
7 Simmer, covered, but stirring occasionally, for about 30–40 minutes, until skins can be crushed easily between finger and thumb.
8 Cut up the peeled fruit, discarding the pips and tough skin.
9 Add pulp and juice to cooked rind.
10 Simmer, covered, 20 minutes longer.
11 Put sugar and 3 pints prepared fruit into large preserving pan, making up the quantity with water if necessary.
12 Heat slowly, stirring occasionally, until the sugar has dissolved.
13 Add a small piece of butter or margarine.
14 Bring to a full rolling boil.
15 Boil for 5 minutes.
16 Remove preserving pan from heat and stir in commercial pectin.
17 Stir and skim by turns for just 7 minutes to cool slightly to prevent fruit floating.
18 Pour into clean hot jars and cover in the usual way.

Seville orange marmalade

cooking time: 1¼ hours

you will need:

8–10 bitter oranges
2 lemons
2 pints water
1 level teaspoon
  bicarbonate of soda

5 lb. sugar
knob of butter
1 bottle commercial
  pectin

Make as previous recipe, steps 1 to 18.

Using your pressure cooker for jams and marmalades

With fruits that take a long time to become tender, it is an excellent idea to use your pressure cooker to soften the fruit for jams or the peel for marmalades. Do not cook for too long a period because one minute under pressure is the equivalent of several minutes cooking in an ordinary saucepan. If you over-cook, you lose both the colour and the flavour of the fruit and you tend to destroy the natural setting properties.

When the fruit has been softened in the pressure cooker, you *must* allow the pressure to drop gradually. You then take off the lid and from then onwards you use your pressure cooker as an ordinary preserving pan.

Lemon marmalade

pressure cooking time: 15 minutes
cooking time in open pan: 25 minutes

you will need:

1 lb. lemons (4
  medium or 3 large
  lemons)

1¼ pints water
2½ lb. sugar

Use method for sweet orange marmalade (see page 51).

Seville or bitter orange marmalade (coarse cut and bitter)

pressure cooking time: 15 minutes
cooking time in open pan: 25 minutes

you will need:

1 lb. oranges or 3 medium sized oranges	1 pint water 2 lb. sugar

1 Wash the oranges well.
2 Put into the pressure cooker with the water.
3 Fix the lid and bring to pressure.
4 Lower the heat.
5 Cook for 15 minutes.
6 Reduce pressure gradually. Remove lid.
7 Remove oranges from the liquid.
8 Allow to cool.
9 Cut up neatly.
10 Put the pips into the liquid.
11 Boil steadily for 10 minutes to extract pectin from them.
12 Remove and replace the cut orange pulp.
13 Bring to the boil.
14 Stir in the warmed sugar.
15 Continue stirring until all the sugar is dissolved.
16 Bring the marmalade to the boil rapidly without stirring until setting point is reached.

Sweet orange marmalade

pressure cooking time: 10 minutes
cooking time in open pan: 25 minutes

you will need:

1 lb. Seville or bitter oranges 1½ pints water 3 lb. sugar	juice 1 lemon or 1 level teaspoon citric or tartaric acid

1 Cut or mince oranges finely, removing pips.
2 Soak peel and pulp overnight in the water, together with the pips, which should be tied up in a piece of muslin.
3 After soaking, put fruit, water and pips in a pressure cooker.
4 Cook for 10 minutes and allow pressure to drop. Remove lid.
5 Take out bag of pips.

6 Stir in warmed sugar and lemon juice or acid. Stir until sugar is dissolved.
7 Bring marmalade to the boil.
8 Boil rapidly until setting point is reached.

Blackcurrant jam

pressure cooking time: 3 minutes
cooking time in open pan: 10 minutes

you will need:

1 lb. blackcurrants ⅜ pint water	1¼ lb. sugar

1 Put fruit and water into pressure cooker.
2 Fix lid, bring to pressure.
3 Lower heat.
4 Cook for 3 minutes.
5 Allow pressure to drop gradually. Remove lid.
6 Stir in sugar.
7 When dissolved boil jam rapidly until set.

Dried peach jam

pressure cooking time: 10 minutes
cooking time in open pan: 10–15 minutes

you will need:

1 lb. dried peaches 1½ pints water 3 lb. sugar	1½ level teaspoons citric or tartaric acid or juice of 1½ lemons

1 Soak the well washed fruit in the water for 48–72 hours.
2 Put into the pressure cooker, without the rack.
3 Fix lid, bring to pressure.
4 Lower heat.
5 Cook for 10 minutes.
6 Allow pressure to drop gradually.
7 Stir in sugar until dissolved and add lemon juice or acid.
8 Boil rapidly for 10–15 minutes.

Green gooseberry jam

pressure cooking time: 1 minute
cooking time in open pan: 10 minutes

you will need:

1 lb. gooseberries 1¼ lb. sugar	¼ pint water

Use method for blackcurrant jam allowing 1 minute only pressure cooking time.

Diabetic preserves

It is possible to make diabetic preserves at home. Samples of these are given and any mixture of fruits can be used. Because you cannot use sugar, which is the ingredient that preserves the fruit in ordinary jam, you must either make small quantities of jam that can be eaten up quickly or you must sterilise the fruit (see page 73).

Sugarless or diabetic jam (using gelatine)

cooking time: 8–15 minutes depending on kind of fruit

you will need:

1 lb. fruit	1 tablespoon hot
little water*	water
8–10 saccharine	½ oz. powdered
tablets	gelatine

*Use ⅛ pint with soft fruit – ¼ pint with firm fruit.

1 Simmer fruit with water until soft.
2 Crush saccharine tablets dissolved in the tablespoon of hot water.
3 Add to the hot but not boiling fruit.
4 Add the gelatine dissolved in the ⅛ pint of hot water.
5 Stir briskly for several minutes.
6 Pour into small jars with firmly fitting tops and seal down.
7 Stand in cool place. This will keep for some days.

Note

To make jam that keeps, pour very hot jam into hot bottling jars. Seal down, giving screw band half turn back. Stand in pan of boiling water and boil briskly for 5 minutes. Lift out and tighten screw band. Test for seal next day by seeing if lid is tight.

Sugarless or diabetic marmalade (using gelatine)

cooking time: 1 hour

you will need:

2 Seville oranges	8 saccharine tablets
2 lemons	¼ oz. gelatine to every
1 pint water	½ pint pulp

1 Cut the rind from the oranges and lemons (being careful to remove no white pith with the rind) and chop it.
2 Cut up the pulp.
3 Place it in a preserving pan with the rind and 1 pint water.
4 Boil gently for about 30 minutes, test carefully.
5 Cook until pulp and rind are tender.
6 Add saccharine.
7 Stir in gelatine dissolved in a little of the hot syrup.
8 Remove from heat.
9 Bottle while still hot.
10 Cover at once.

Do not make large quantities as this will not keep unless you sterilise (see page 73).

Diabetic marmalade (with Sorbitol)

cooking time: approximately 2¼ hours

you will need:

1 lb. Seville oranges	2 tablespoons lemon
2 pints water	juice
2 lb. Sorbitol powder	

1 Simmer the oranges in the water until very soft.
2 Remove fruit from the water, cut in halves.
3 Take out the pips, simmer these in the liquid in the pan for 15 minutes, then strain.
4 Return the liquid to the pan with the neatly sliced or minced orange peel and pulp.
5 Heat again, add the Sorbitol and lemon juice.
6 Stir until the Sorbitol has dissolved, then boil rapidly until setting point is reached.
7 Cool slightly. Stir to distribute the peel, then put into jars and cover in the usual way.

Diabetic jams (with Sorbitol) without commercial pectin

The ingredients for these jams vary slightly according to whether the fruit being used is rich or poor in pectin.

cooking time: 25–35 minutes

you will need:

Fruits rich in pectin	*Fruits poor in pectin*
1 lb. blackcurrants or cooking apples, gooseberries or damsons	1 lb. blackberries or cherries, strawberries or apricots
1 lb. 2 oz. Sorbitol powder	14 oz. Sorbitol powder
8–12 tablespoons water depending on juiciness of fruit	2 tablespoons lemon juice
	little, if any, water

1 Simmer the fruit with the water or, for fruit poor in pectin, heat the fruit gently until juices flow, then continue simmering until soft.
2 Add the Sorbitol, stir until dissolved, and pour in the lemon juice (if used).
3 Boil rapidly until jam reaches 220–222°F. or wrinkles when a little is put on a saucer to cool.
4 Cool slightly, stir briskly, then put into small jars. Cover tightly and seal.

Note

For any other fruits, providing they are not over ripe, use 1 lb. Sorbitol and 1 tablespoon lemon juice to 1 lb. prepared fruit.

Diabetic jams (with Sorbitol) using commercial pectin

This is another method of making diabetic jams, using a Sorbitol product.

cooking time: 25–35 minutes

you will need:

2½ lb. fruit	2½ lb. Sorbitol powder
¼ pint water with firm fruit – damsons, hard plums, etc:	knob butter
⅛ pint water with moderately soft fruit – ripe gooseberries, etc:	½ bottle commercial pectin
no water with soft fruit – raspberries, etc.	5 saccharine tablets
	½ oz. gelatine

1 Put the fruit and water in the preserving pan.
2 Simmer until soft, removing stones with a perforated spoon.
3 Stir in the Sorbitol and bring to the boil, adding the butter.
4 Boil hard for 1 minute.
5 Remove from the heat and stir in the commercial pectin, saccharin tablets and the gelatine dissolved in ⅛ pint very hot water.
6 Stir thoroughly until blended.
7 Pour into jar while hot and seal down.
   In order to keep, this jam must be covered immediately with a very good seal, either a bottling top or melted paraffin wax.

Fruit curds

It must be remembered that you are adding eggs to very acid ingredients in a fruit curd. This is why stress is laid on the fact that the curd must thicken *slowly*. If by chance it shows signs of curdling, lift the mixture off the heat and whisk very sharply for a few minutes. This should get rid of the curdled effect and you can then replace over heat to finish cooking. Remember the mixture thickens quite a lot as it cools, so do not over-cook.

Lemon curd

cooking time: 30 minutes

you will need:

rind 3 lemons	4 oz. fresh butter
juice 2 large lemons	2 eggs
8 oz. sugar	

1 Grate the rind carefully, removing just the yellow 'zest', but none of the white pith. If using loaf sugar, rub this over the lemons until all the yellow has been removed. *continued*

2 Squeeze the juice from the fruit.

3 Put all the ingredients – except eggs – into double saucepan or basin over hot water.

4 Cook stirring from time to time, until butter and sugar have melted.

5 Add the well beaten eggs.

6 Continue cooking until the mixture coats the back of a wooden spoon.

7 Pour into jars and seal down in the usual way.

Apple and lemon curd

cooking time: 1½ hours

you will need:

2 large cooking apples	4 oz. fresh butter
8 oz. sugar	2 eggs
rind 3 lemons	juice 2 large lemons

1 Bake the apples in their jackets so that you soften them without adding any water.

2 Remove the pulp and beat until smooth.

3 Mix the lemon rind, etc., and proceed as for lemon curd.

Note

This has a slightly lower percentage of sugar in the completed preserve, so is not meant to keep quite as long. To keep indefinitely, increase amount of sugar to 1 lb. It does, however, make a more economical preserve than lemon curd.

Grapefruit curd

cooking time: 30 minutes

you will need:

grated rind 2 large grapefruits	8 oz. sugar
Juice 2 large grapefruits	4 oz. fresh butter
	2 eggs

Use method for lemon curd.

Orange curd

cooking time: 30 minutes

you will need:

rind 3 oranges	4 oz. fresh butter
juice 2 large oranges	2 eggs
8 oz. sugar	

1 Grate the rind carefully, removing just the yellow 'zest' but none of the white pith. If

using loaf sugar, rub this over the oranges until all the yellow has been removed.

2 Squeeze the juice from the fruit.

3 Put all ingredients – except eggs – into a double saucepan or basin over hot water.

4 Cook, stirring from time to time, until the butter and sugar have melted.

5 Add the well beaten eggs and continue cooking until the mixture coats the back of a wooden spoon.

6 Pour into jars and seal down in the usual way.

Orange and lemon curd

cooking time: 30 minutes

you will need:

rind 1 lemon	4 oz. fresh butter
rind 2 oranges	or margarine
juice 2 large oranges	2 eggs
8 oz. castor or loaf sugar	

Use method for lemon curd.

Marrow curd (1)

cooking time: 45 minutes

you will need:

To each lb. cooked marrow pulp *add*

grated rind and juice 2 lemons	4 oz. butter
1 lb. sugar	2 eggs

1 Peel the marrow and remove skin and seeds.

2 Put into a pan with just enough water to cover the bottom.

3 Cook until quite soft.

4 Measure the pulp and add other ingredients (proportion see above).

5 Put altogether into a double saucepan.

6 Cook until very smooth.

Marrow curd (2)

cooking time: about 45 minutes

you will need:

marrow	sugar
lemons	butter

Peel vegetable marrow, remove the seeds. To each 1 lb. of marrow, allow the finely grated rind of 1 large lemon, the juice of 1 large lemon and 1 lb. of sugar and 1 oz. of butter, see note. Steam the marrow until nearly soft, put into a preserving pan or saucepan, add the lemon rind and cook over a very low heat until very soft, adding the butter. When very soft add the sugar, stir until dissolved, then add the lemon juice and boil steadily until set.

Note

If you wish to double the amount of lemon and butter you can do so.

Marrow lemon curd

cooking time: 30 minutes

you will need:

8 oz. cooked sieved marrow	8 oz. sugar
rind 3 lemons	4 oz. fresh butter
juice 2 large lemons	2 eggs

1 Simmer the marrow so no water is added, strain and beat or sieve until smooth. Add to lemon rind, etc.
2 Continue as for lemon curd.

Tangerine curd

cooking time: 30 minutes

you will need:

grated rind and juice 6 tangerines	5 oz. fresh butter
juice 1 lemon	3 medium sized eggs or 2 large eggs
10 oz. sugar	

Use method for lemon curd (see page 53).

Parsley honey

cooking time: about 1 hour

you will need:

2 large handfuls of fresh parsley (about 4–5 oz.)	1½ pints water
	1 lb. sugar
	1 dessertspoon vinegar

1 Wash and pick over the parsley.

2 Chop up with stalks, roughly.
3 Put into a pan with the water.
4 Bring to the boil.
5 Boil gently until the water is reduced to 1 pint.
6 Save this pint. Rinse out the saucepan.
7 Pour in the strained parsley water.
8 Add the warmed sugar.
9 When dissolved bring to the boil.
10 Add the vinegar and boil slowly until a little, when tested on a plate, is of a clear honey consistency, which will probably take about 30 minutes.
11 Pot and seal in the usual way.

Fruit butters

1 To make a fruit butter follow any of the directions for jam up to the point when the sugar is added.
2 Rub the fruit purée through a sieve.
3 Measure and add 8 oz. sugar to every lb. or pint of pulp.
4 Boil until thickened.
5 Allow to cool.

Fruit butters are generally served as a sweet with ice cream, etc., and because of the low content of sugar will not keep like a jam or a cheese. If you wish it to keep, then add extra sugar when, of course, it becomes exactly like a cheese. Alternatively, you can pour it into bottling jars and preserve it like pulped fruit (see pages 73, 74).

Apple butter	– follow method for fruit butter.
Apricot butter	– follow method for fruit butter.
Greengage butter	– follow method for fruit butter.
Gooseberry butter	– follow method for fruit butter.
Peach butter	– follow method for fruit butter.
Plum butter	– follow method for fruit butter.
Raspberry butter	– follow method for fruit butter.
Strawberry butter	– follow method for fruit butter.

Pickles

1 Always use very good quality vegetables – firm and not discoloured.
2 Use pure malt vinegar – white vinegar if preferred.
3 Cover well – see point 5 in chutneys (see page 60).
4 Never use copper, brass or iron pans.
5 You must see the vegetables are completely covered with vinegar.
6 It is essential to put vegetables in brine before covering with vinegar. (For brine recipes see this page and page 57.)
7 You should boil vinegar before using, even when allowing it to become cold afterwards – see spiced vinegar, this page.

Pickled beetroot

cooking time: 10 minutes for beetroot
15 minutes for vinegar

1 Cut the cooked beetroot into slices or cubes as desired.
2 Put into boiling salted water (1 tablespoon salt to 1 pint water).
3 Simmer gently for about 10 minutes being careful not to break slices.
4 Drain and pack into jars.
5 Cover with hot spiced vinegar, i.e. white malt or ordinary malt vinegar boiled with pickling spices. Use 1 tablespoon pickling spices to each pint vinegar.
6 Seal down at once.
7 Store in a cool dark place.

Pickled capers

1 Put the capers into brine made with 2 oz. kitchen salt to 1 pint water.
2 Leave for 24 hours.
3 Drain but do not wash.
4 Put into jars and pour over hot spiced white vinegar.
5 Cover thoroughly.

Pickled red cabbage

cooking time: 15 minutes to make spiced vinegar

1 Cut the cabbage into shreds.
2 Put into a basin with a good sprinkling of salt between each layer.
3 Leave for 24 hours.
4 Drain thoroughly.
5 Pack into jars and pour over the cold spiced vinegar. For quantities of spiced vinegar, see pickled cucumbers.
6 Seal at once.

Pickled cucumbers

1 If the cucumbers are very small, they can be left whole, but otherwise cut into convenient sized pieces.
2 Put into wet brine, or cover with salt (dry brine) and leave overnight.
3 Prepare spiced vinegar.
4 Strain spiced vinegar and cool.
5 Remove the cucumber from the brine and rinse well under the cold tap.
6 Drain thoroughly.
7 Pack into jars.
8 Pour over the cold vinegar and seal carefully.

Wet brine

Always use household salt, not the free-flowing table salt. Unless stated to the contrary, use 2 oz. salt to 1 pint cold water.

Spiced vinegar

Unless stated to the contrary, this mixture of spices and vinegar gives a very good result for most pickles. Buy the pickling spice from the grocer and you will find they consist of a mixture of chillis, peppercorns, cloves etc. To each pint vinegar: 1 level tablespoon mixed pickling spice. Boil together for 15 minutes, strain then use as directed in the recipe.

Dry brine

You will have a 'crisper' texture for pickled cucumbers if you use dry brine, but many people prefer the softer texture given by soaking in wet brine. Sprinkle layers of kitchen salt between layers of shredded cabbage or sliced or whole small cucumbers – leave for 24 hours, then shake away surplus salt.

Sweet pickled cucumbers

cooking time: 15 minutes to make spiced vinegar

Use the method for pickled cucumbers, but add 1–2 teaspoons sugar to each pint pickled vinegar.

Pickled cauliflower

cooking time: 15 minutes to make spiced vinegar

1 Break the cauliflower into neat flowerets.
2 Leave in brine (see before) for 24 hours.
3 Drain well and rinse in cold water.
4 Cover with cold spiced vinegar.

Sweet pickled cauliflower

cooking time: 15 minutes to make spiced vinegar

Use recipe for pickled cauliflower but allow 1 teaspoon sugar to each $\frac{1}{2}$ pint of spiced vinegar.

Pickled damsons

cooking time: 25–30 minutes

you will need:

2 pints vinegar	3–4 lb. sugar,
1 tablespoon pickling	preferably brown
spice	8 lb. damsons

1 Boil the spices and vinegar for about 10 minutes.
2 Strain them, or tie the spices in muslin bag and put into the vinegar.
3 Stir in the sugar and when dissolved add fruit.

4 Simmer *gently* until very soft, but quite unbroken.
5 Lift out the fruit, remove spices and pack fruit into jars.
6 Boil the vinegar and sugar until slightly syrupy.
7 Pour over the fruit and seal down.
8 Store for several months before serving.

Pickled gherkins

cooking time: 15 minutes to make spiced vinegar

When gherkins are obtainable, pickle in the same way as cucumbers (see page 56).

Pickled marrow

cooking time: 10 minutes

you will need:

2 lb. marrow (after peeling)	$\frac{1}{4}$ oz. curry powder
4 oz. salt	6 peppercorns
4 oz. sugar	$\frac{3}{4}$ pint vinegar
$\frac{1}{4}$ oz. ground ginger	$\frac{3}{4}$ oz. mustard

1 Cut up the marrow, sprinkle with salt and allow to stand overnight.
2 Add other ingredients to the vinegar.
3 Boil for 5 minutes, then add drained and rinsed marrow.
4 Cook until tender.
5 Pack pickle into jars and seal.

Pickled mushrooms

cooking time: 5 minutes mushrooms
5 minutes for vinegar

you will need:

1 lb. small button mushrooms	1 level teaspoon black pepper
1 oz. salt	$\frac{1}{4}$ teaspoon ground mace
2 pints vinegar	

1 Peel or rub off the skin of the mushrooms with the help of a little salt.
2 Throw into boiling water with plenty of salt and boil for 5 minutes.
3 Pack into jars and pour the vinegar over them while boiling, the pepper and spice having been boiled with the vinegar.
4 White vinegar is the best for this purpose and the mushrooms will keep for a fairly long period.

Mixed vinegar pickles

cooking time: 15 minutes for spiced vinegar

Choose small onions, flowerets of cauliflower, green beans, pieces of cucumber or gherkin, green tomatoes. Prepare as for pickled cucumbers (see page 56), arranging an attractive assortment of the vegetables in the jars. It gives both colour and extra flavour if the chillis are left in the spiced vinegar.

Pickled nasturtium seeds

cooking time: 10 minutes for boiling vinegar

you will need:

to each pint vinegar add ½ oz. salt and 6 peppercorns	nasturtium seeds vinegar to cover them

1 Boil the vinegar, salt and peppercorns together
2 When cold, strain into a wide necked bottle.
3 Gather the seeds on a dry day.
4 Put them into the vinegar and cork closely.

Note

These pickled seeds form an excellent substitute for capers. They are ready for use in about 3 months but may be kept for much longer.

Pickled onions or shallots

cooking time: 15 minutes to spice vinegar

1 Remove outer skins from the onions or shallots, using a stainless knife to prevent them discolouring.
2 Soak in brine for 36–48 hours. For quantities see page 56.
3 Then proceed as for pickled cucumbers (see page 56).

Piccalilli

cooking time: 15–20 minutes

1 Use exactly the same ingredients as for mustard pickles.
2 Chop the pieces of vegetables rather smaller than for mustard pickles so that you get a greater blending of these in the mustard sauce.

Mustard pickles

cooking time: 15–20 minutes

you will need:

2 lb. mixed vegetables, e.g. cauliflower, marrow, onions, cucumber, small green tomatoes, beans, brine (see page 56) 1 pint vinegar 1 tablespoon pickling spice	1 tablespoon mustard powder ½ tablespoon turmeric powder 2 oz. sugar 1 tablespoon flour or ½ tablespoon cornflour 1 dessertspoon ginger

1 Cut the vegetables into neat pieces.
2 Soak overnight in brine.
3 Wash well under the cold tap and drain thoroughly.
4 Boil the vinegar and pickling spice together for 10 minutes.
5 Mix all dry ingredients with a very little vinegar until a smooth paste.
6 Pour over the strained hot vinegar and stir well.
7 Return to the pan and cook until just thickened.
8 Put in the vegetables and cook for 5 minutes.
9 Put into jars and seal well.

Pickled cocktail onions

cooking time: 15 minutes to spice vinegar

1 Choose very tiny onions indeed and pickle as for pickled onions.
2 Some people like to add a little colouring to the spiced vinegar to colour the onions, but this is a matter of taste.
3 To keep them very white, use a white wine vinegar and you may like to add 1 or 2 teaspoons sugar for sweet pickled onions.

Sweet pickled onions

cooking time: 15 minutes for spiced vinegar

Ordinary or cocktail onions can all be put into a sweet vinegar. Allow 1–2 teaspoons of sugar to each ½ pint of vinegar.

Sweet pickles

cooking time: 15–20 minutes

you will need:

2 lb. mixed vegetables, e.g. cauliflower, marrow, onion, cucumber, small green tomatoes, beans	1 pint vinegar
	1 tablespoon pickling spice
	6 oz. sugar
	2 level tablespoons flour or 1 level tablespoon cornflour
brine (see page 56)	

Follow Mustard pickles recipe, steps 1 to 9. If desired, 4-6 oz. sultanas can be added with vegetables for cooking.

Pickled walnuts

cooking time: 15 minutes to spice vinegar

1 Be certain nuts are not over-ripe.
2 Prick deeply with a silver fork in 2 or 3 places.
3 Soak in wet brine (see page 56) for at least 3 days.
4 Remove from brine and place on a tray or cloth in the sun, moving occasionally.
5 Slowly they will turn black, this will take 2 or 3 days (if very hot 24 hours may suffice).
6 When quite black, pack into jars and cover with cold spiced vinegar (see page 56).
7 Tie down and leave to mature for at least 1 month before use.

Sweet pickled walnuts

cooking time: 15 minutes for spiced vinegar

Use method for pickled walnuts, but add 1–2 teaspoons sugar to the spiced vinegar.

Pickled hard-boiled eggs

cooking time: 15 minutes for eggs

1 Hard-boil eggs by placing in cold water, bringing to the boil then turning out the heat, covering the pan and leaving for 15 minutes.
2 Take out the eggs and immediately plunge them into cold running water so that they cool rapidly.
3 Shell eggs and remove any skin.
4 When quite cold place the eggs in an ordinary glass jam jar and cover with cold vinegar.
5 Leave for a day or so before using.

Pickled fruits

cooking time: 15 minutes to make spiced vinegar, then further 10–25 minutes

you will need:

1 dessertspoon pickling spice	1 lb. sugar
½ pint white vinegar to keep the colour of the fruit	2 lb. pears, peaches, crab apples, damsons, plums or apricots

1 Tie spices in muslin and simmer in the vinegar for 10 minutes.
2 Strain.
3 Add the sugar to the vinegar.
4 Bring to the boil and simmer until the sugar has dissolved.
5 Put the fruit – peeled and cut into quarters or halves – into the vinegar syrup and simmer gently until just tender. Crab apples and damsons should be left whole.
6 Take out the fruit and pack into bottling jars.
7 Boil the vinegar (with the lid off the pan) for a few minutes to thicken liquid.
8 Pour over the fruit and seal down at once.
9 Do not use metal tops next to the vinegar otherwise they will rust. Bottling jars are ideal.

Spiced fruits

cooking time: as pickled fruit

1 These are particularly good when pickling apples and pears.
2 Use recipe for pickled fruits, but use ordinary malt vinegar and add little mixed spice, cinnamon bark and nutmeg to the vinegar and sugar.
3 Cut apples into fairly thick slices and halve pears.
4 Sliced lemons can be pickled in the same way and are very good with cold duck or pork. Do not remove peel but take out pips.

Spiced dried fruits

cooking time: 10–15 minutes to make spiced vinegar. Approximately 1 hour for fruit

you will need:

2 lb. mixed dried fruit (prunes, dried apricots, peaches, figs)	2 pints spiced vinegar (see page 56)
	8 oz. sugar

1 Wash the dried fruit and soak overnight in the vinegar.
2 Add the sugar.
3 Simmer until soft but unbroken.
4 Pack into jars and seal down.

Chutneys and relishes

1 Do not attempt to cut down on the quantity of sugar or vinegar in a chutney recipe as this is the preservative.
2 Don't put in all the vinegar at once as this rather takes away the flavour of the ingredients – put in about ¼ of the vinegar, then add rest gradually during the cooking period.
3 Cook chutney with lid OFF pan so it thickens – stir from time to time.
4 Pour the chutney into jars while still hot – filling to neck of jar.
5 Cover very well – bottling jars are ideal as they have glass lids. Never put metal tops directly next to the chutney otherwise the vinegar in the chutney will spoil both taste and colour and will make the lid rust and be very difficult to remove. You can buy special pickling jars or instead put a round of waxed paper on chutney – then a thin layer of melted wax (paraffin wax) then the final cover *or* put the waxed paper then several thicknesses of brown or parchment paper over this – tying it down tightly.
6 Always use pure malt vinegar – white vinegar can be used for light coloured chutneys if desired and to retain bright colour.
7 Store in cool dry place – preferably in dark – to keep well.

8 Never use copper, brass or iron pans; aluminium is excellent.

Apple chutney

cooking time: 40 minutes

you will need:

1 lb. onions (grated or finely chopped)	1 teaspoon pickling spice
½ pint vinegar	1 teaspoon salt
2 lb. apples (after peeling and coring), chopped	1 teaspoon ground ginger
2–4 oz. dried fruit (if liked)	12 oz. sugar

1 Put the onion into a saucepan with ⅛ pint vinegar and simmer until nearly soft.
2 Add the chopped apples, dried fruit, spices (tied securely in a muslin bag), salt, ground ginger and just enough vinegar to stop the mixture from burning.
3 Cook gently until the fruit is soft, stirring from time to time.
4 Add remainder of the vinegar and thoroughly stir in the sugar.
5 Boil steadily until the chutney is thick.
6 Remove pickling spices.
7 Pour into hot jars.

Apricot chutney

cooking time: 50 minutes

you will need:

8 oz. dried apricots
1 pint vinegar (white vinegar is good but not essential)
4 oz. raisins (stoned), chopped
4 oz. sultanas
3 teaspoons pickling spice
1 good teaspoon salt
2 cloves garlic
juice and peel 1 lemon
1 lb. apples (after peeling and coring)
1 lb. brown sugar

1 Cut dried apricots into small pieces and soak for 2–3 hours in cold water.
2 Drain and put into saucepan with a little of the vinegar and all the other ingredients except apples and sugar.
3 The pickling spice should be tied in muslin.
4 Boil steadily for 30 minutes, adding vinegar, then add grated or chopped apples and sugar.
5 Stir until sugar dissolves.
6 Boil for about another 20 minutes or until it thickens.
7 Remove pickling spices.
8 Put into hot jars and cover as directed.

Apple and mint chutney

cooking time: 40 minutes

Use recipe and method for apple chutney but allow 1 dessertspoon of chopped mint to each lb. chutney. Stir this in just before putting into bottles.

Aubergine chutney

cooking time: 1 hour

you will need:

2 teaspoons pickling spice
2 lb. aubergines (unpeeled)
12 oz. onions
1 lb. cooking apples (after peeling and coring)
2 teaspoons ginger
1 teaspoon salt
½ pint vinegar
1¼ lb. brown sugar

1 Tie the spices in a muslin bag.
2 Wipe and cut aubergines into thin slices.
3 Put all the ingredients except the sugar into a saucepan – chopping the onions very finely.

4 Simmer gently until tender.
5 Remove the bag of spices and stir in the sugar.
6 Boil until thick.
7 Put into hot jars and seal down.

Variations

With lemon – a little grated lemon rind gives a good flavour.
With peppers – a mixture of aubergines and red and green peppers instead of all aubergines is excellent.

Aubergine and capsicum chutney

cooking time: 30 minutes

you will need:

4 medium sized aubergines (peeled)
4 medium sized capsicums (or sweet red peppers)
salt to taste
little turmeric or saffron powder
1 dessertspoon good Indian curry powder
¾ pint malt or wine vinegar
2-inch piece cinnamon
1-inch piece ginger
1–2 bay leaves, if liked
little olive oil
4 oz. peeled sliced shallots
1 or 2 small cloves garlic (peeled), finely sliced
little brown sugar or two peeled chopped apples, if liked

1 Cut the aubergines and peppers into slices lengthwise and then into smaller pieces.
2 Rub these over with salt and saffron.
3 Dissolve and mix the curry powder into a tablespoon or two of the vinegar and put in the cinnamon and ginger and bay leaves.
4 Leave for 15 minutes.
5 Heat the olive oil and fry the cut vegetables, sliced shallots (or onion) and garlic for about 10 minutes in a large frying pan or saucepan, stirring and turning it over every now and again; add sugar or apples, if used.
6 Add the curry mixture and blend all together well and cook over a low fire for about 10 minutes, stirring gently a few times.
7 Add rest of the vinegar, simmer for a few more minutes until thick.
8 Taste for salt and if liked 'hot' add a little cayenne pepper or paprika.
9 Put into dry, wide mouthed jars when slightly warm, first removing cinnamon, ginger and bay leaves.

Autumn fruit chutney

cooking time: 1½ hours

you will need:

2 lb. plums (stoned)	½ teaspoon mace
2 lb. cooking apples (after peeling and coring)	½ teaspoon mixed spice
	2 oz. root ginger
2 lb. tomatoes	1 lb. sultanas
2 lb. onions	1 pint vinegar – good measure
1–2 cloves garlic	
1 oz. salt	1 lb. Demerara sugar
¼ teaspoon cayenne	

1 Chop all the fruit and vegetables. Add spice, etc.
2 Boil in the vinegar until tender.
3 Add the sugar and continue cooking until thick.

Beetroot chutney

cooking time: 40 minutes

you will need:

1 lb. onions, chopped	2 teaspoons salt
1 pint spiced white vinegar	1 lb. apples
	1 lb. white sugar
3 lb. cooked beetroot	

1 Cook the chopped onions for a short time in a little of the vinegar.
2 Add the rest of the ingredients and proceed as for apple chutney (see page 60).
The beetroot should be diced in very small pieces.

Variation

With sultanas – 8 oz. light coloured sultanas could be added to this recipe.

Blackberry chutney

cooking time: 1¼ hours

you will need:

1 lb. cooking apples (unpeeled)	1 teaspoon powdered mace
12 oz. onions	1 pint vinegar (preferably white)
3 lb. blackberries	
3 teaspoons salt	1 lb. brown sugar
½ oz. mustard	
2 teaspoons powdered ginger	

1 Peel, core and chop the apples and onions.
2 Put into a pan with the blackberries, salt, spices and ¼ pint vinegar and cook for 1 hour adding rest of vinegar gradually.
3 Rub through a sieve to remove the pips.
4 Add sugar and cook until the desired consistency is obtained.

Blackberry and apple chutney

cooking time: 1¼ hours

Use ingredients for blackberry chutney, but use 2 lb. blackberries and 2 lb. apples. Proceed as for blackberry chutney.

Cherry chutney

cooking time: 40–60 minutes

Follow the recipe and method for damson chutney, using rather tart cherries – morello cherries are ideal. When the chutney is thick, add approximately 8 oz. chopped nuts.

Cranberry chutney

cooking time: 40 minutes to 1 hour

you will need:

1 lb. cooking apples	1 teaspoon salt
1 lb. cranberries	½ pint vinegar
6 oz. raisins	2 teaspoons pickling spice
1 teaspoon mixed spice	
	8 oz. sugar

1 Put the chopped apples, cranberries, dried fruit, spices tied in muslin, salt, in a pan with just enough vinegar to stop the mixture burning.
2 Cook gently until the fruit is soft, stirring from time to time.
3 Add the remainder of the vinegar and the sugar.
4 Stir until the sugar is dissolved.
5 Boil steadily until thick.
6 Remove pickling spices and pour into hot jars and seal down.

Damson chutney

cooking time: 1¼ hours

you will need:

3 lb. damsons
2 pints vinegar
1½ lb. cooking apples
    (after peeling and
    coring), chopped
1 lb. onions (peeled),
    chopped

2 teaspoons ginger
1 oz. pickling spice
3 teaspoons salt
1 lb. sugar

1 Simmer damsons in 1 pint vinegar until tender enough to remove stones.
2 Add chopped apples, onions, ginger, pickling spices (tied in muslin) and salt.
3 Continue cooking until fruit is completely soft.
4 Add rest of vinegar and sugar.
5 Boil steadily until thick.
6 Put into hot jars and seal down.

Quick date chutney

cooking time: 10–15 minutes to make spiced vinegar

you will need:

1 lb. dates
1 small onion
seasoning
about ¼ pint spiced
    vinegar

good pinch
    ginger and/or
    mixed spice

1 Chop dates finely.
2 Add little finely chopped onion, seasoning.
3 Pour over enough hot spiced vinegar to moisten.
4 Stir in good pinch ginger and/or mixed spice.
5 Stir well until the dates are softened.
6 Use fresh, as this does not keep.

Elderberry chutney

cooking time: 40 minutes to 1 hour

Use recipe and method for apple chutney (see page 60) but use 1 lb. apples and 1 lb. elderberries.
This is very pleasant if a little cayenne pepper is added.

Gooseberry chutney

cooking time: 40 minutes to 1 hour

you will need:

2 lb. gooseberries
8 oz. cooking apples
1 teaspoon salt
½ pint vinegar
1 teaspoon pickling
    spice

1 lb. onions (grated or
    finely chopped)
12 oz. sugar
1 teaspoon ground
    ginger
2–4 oz. dried fruit (if
    liked)

Use method for apple chutney (see page 60).

Lemon chutney

cooking time: 1½ hours

you will need:

4 large or 6 small
    lemons
8 oz. onions
1 oz. salt
¾ pint malt
    vinegar
1 lb. granulated
    sugar

4 oz. seedless raisins
1 oz. mustard seed
    (well crushed)
1 teaspoon ground
    ginger
½ small teaspoon
    cayenne pepper

1 Wash lemons.
2 Slice thinly and remove all pips.
3 Peel and chop onions.
4 Put on to a dish with the sliced lemons and sprinkle with salt.
5 Leave for 24 hours.
6 Put in a preserving pan, add all the other ingredients.
7 Bring to the boil.
8 Simmer until quite tender and of the consistency of chutney.
9 Turn into dry jars and tie down when cold.

Mango chutney

cooking time: 50 minutes

you will need:

2 teaspoons pickling
 spice
12 oz. onions (peeled),
 sliced
2 lb. mangoes

1 lb. cooking apples
 (after peeling and
 coring), sliced
2 teaspoons ginger
1 pint vinegar
1¼ lb. brown sugar

1 Tie the spices in a bag.
2 Chop the onions in very small pieces.
3 Put all ingredients with a little vinegar into a
 pan, except the sugar.
4 Simmer gently until soft, adding vinegar gradually.
5 Remove the bag of spices.
6 Add the sugar and boil until thick.
7 It is advisable to keep the pieces of mango fairly
 large.
8 Some people may like a little salt in this chutney,
 but it is generally a sweet, rather hot chutney.
9 Turn into dry jars and seal when cold.

Marrow chutney

cooking time: 40 minutes

Use recipe and method for apple chutney (see
page 60) but use marrow instead of apple and
increase ginger to taste.

Orange chutney

cooking time: 1½ hours

Use the recipe and method for lemon chutney
(see page 63), but allow 4 really large oranges
instead of lemons.

Orange and lemon chutney

cooking time: 1¼–1½ hours

you will need:

3 large lemons
2 medium oranges
1 pint spiced vinegar
 (spiced white vinegar
 may be used to give
 a clearer colour)
8 oz. onions
6 oz. light coloured
 sultanas

1 teaspoon powdered
 ginger
salt to taste
1 teaspoon cinnamon
little pepper
1 lb. castor sugar

1 Wash lemons and oranges and squeeze out the
 juice.
2 Mince or shred peel and pulp, etc. of fruit (as
 for marmalade) and discard pips.
3 Soak for 24 hours in the cold spiced vinegar.
4 Next day add juice and thinly sliced onions.
5 Simmer very gently until peel and onions are
 tender.
6 Add sultanas, seasoning, etc. to taste, together
 with sugar.
7 Cook until thick.

Plum chutney

cooking time: 40 minutes

you will need:

2 lb. plums
2–4 oz. dried fruit
 (if desired)
1 tablespoon pickling
 spice

1 teaspoon salt
1 teaspoon ground
 ginger
½ pint vinegar
12 oz. sugar

1 Simmer stoned plums, dried fruit, pickling
 spice (tied securely in muslin bag), salt and
 ginger in a saucepan with just enough vinegar
 to stop the mixture from burning.
2 Cook gently until the fruit is soft, stirring from
 time to time.
3 Add remainder of vinegar and thoroughly stir
 in sugar.
4 Boil steadily until the mixture is thick.
5 Remove spices.
6 Pour chutney into hot jars and seal.

Plum chutney (minted)

Add ½ tablespoon chopped mint to chutney
before putting into jars.

Pear chutney

cooking time: 1½ hours

Use recipe and method for autumn fruit chutney (see page 62) but use pears instead of plums.

Red pepper chutney

cooking time: 50 minutes

you will need:

2 cloves garlic
4 capsicums (sweet red peppers)
2 aubergines (eggplants)
2 good sized cooking apples (peeled and cored)
8 oz. onions
¼ oz. root ginger
6 chillis
½–1 tablespoon curry powder
1 teaspoon saffron powder
1 pint spiced vinegar
salt to taste
2 oz. brown sugar
6 oz. raisins (optional)

1 Crush the cloves of garlic well.
2 Slice the peppers (removing the seeds) and the aubergines, apples and onions.
3 Tie the root ginger and chillis in muslin.
4 Blend the curry powder and saffron with a little vinegar.
5 Add other seasoning.
6 Proceed as apple chutney (see page 60).

Red pepper relish

cooking time: 30 minutes

you will need:

12 capsicums (sweet red peppers)
12 green peppers
12 onions
1¼ pints vinegar
12 oz. brown sugar
2 tablespoons salt
2 tablespoons celery seeds

1 Chop the peppers, discarding all seeds, and chop the onions.
2 Simmer in the vinegar until tender, adding sugar, salt and celery seed tied in muslin.
3 Pour into jars and seal as chutney (see page 60).

Rhubarb chutney

cooking time: 35–40 minutes

Use recipe and method for apple chutney (see page 60) but use 3 lb. rhubarb instead of apples, but if liked the quantity of dried ginger can be increased to 2 level teaspoons.

Rhubarb chutney (minted)

Make as before and stir in ½ tablespoon chopped mint before pouring into jars.

Spanish tomato chutney

cooking time: 25–30 minutes

you will need:

3 lb. green tomatoes (skinned)
1 red pepper
1 lb. onions
2 tablespoons salt
1½ pints vinegar
1 teaspoon mixed spice
1 teaspoon peppercorns
1 teaspoon mustard seed
few chillis
1 teaspoon cloves
12 oz. sugar

1 Slice the tomatoes and red pepper, and chop onions finely.
2 Sprinkle with salt and leave for several hours.
3 Drain well.
4 Put into a preserving pan with the vinegar and spices tied in muslin.
5 Simmer steadily for 10 minutes.
6 Add the sugar and continue simmering for another 15–20 minutes.
7 Pour into jars and seal down.
This is less soft than an ordinary chutney.

Tomato chutney

cooking time: 40 minutes with ripe tomatoes,
50–55 minutes with green tomatoes

you will need:

1 teaspoon pickling spice	1 rounded teaspoon mustard powder
8 oz. finely chopped onions	$\frac{1}{2}$ teaspoon ginger
$\frac{1}{2}$ pint malt vinegar	$\frac{1}{2}$ teaspoon salt
8 oz. apples, peeled and cored	$\frac{1}{4}$ teaspoon pepper
2 lb. tomatoes, green or red	8 oz. sultanas
	8 oz. sugar

1 Put the pickling spices into a piece of muslin.
2 Put the onion into a saucepan with 2–3 table-spoons vinegar and simmer gently until nearly soft.
3 Add the chopped apples, skinned sliced toma-toes, spices, salt, pepper, mustard, ginger and sultanas.
4 Simmer gently until all the mixture is quite soft, stirring from time to time.
5 Add the remainder of the vinegar and the sugar.
6 When the sugar has quite dissolved boil steadily until the chutney is the consistency of jam.
7 Remove the little bag of spice.
8 Pour the hot chutney into warm jars and seal down at once.

Green tomato chutney (1)

cooking time: 50 minutes

you will need:

8 oz. onions, grated or finely chopped	2 lb. green tomatoes (skinned)
$\frac{1}{2}$ pint vinegar	1 teaspoon pickling spice
8 oz. apples (after peeling and coring)	$\frac{1}{2}$ teaspoon salt
	8 oz. sugar

1 Put the onion into a saucepan with $\frac{1}{8}$ pint vin-egar.
2 Simmer until nearly soft.
3 Chop the apples and add the chopped tomatoes, spices (tied in a muslin bag) and salt and just enough vinegar to stop the mixture from burning.
4 Cook gently until tomatoes and apples are soft, stirring from time to time.
5 Add remainder of vinegar and stir in sugar.
6 Boil steadily until the chutney is thick.
7 Remove spices, pour into hot jars and seal.

Green tomato chutney (minted)

Follow previous recipe and stir in $\frac{1}{2}$ tablespoon chopped mint before pouring into jars.

Red tomato and apple chutney

cooking time: 40 minutes

you will need:

$1\frac{1}{2}$ lb. red tomatoes	1 teaspoon pickling spice
8 oz. onions, grated or finely chopped	1 teaspoon salt
$\frac{1}{2}$ pint vinegar (brown or white)	1 teaspoon ground ginger
$1\frac{1}{2}$ lb. apples (after peeling and coring)	4 oz. dried fruit
	12 oz. sugar

1 Skin the tomatoes.
2 Put onion into a saucepan with $\frac{1}{8}$ pint vinegar and simmer until nearly soft.
3 Chop apples and tomatoes, add spice (tied securely in a muslin bag), the salt, ground ginger, dried fruit and just enough vinegar to stop the mixture from burning.
4 Cook gently until the fruit is soft, stirring from time to time.
5 Add the remainder of the vinegar and tho-roughly stir in the sugar.
6 Boil steadily until the chutney is thick.
7 Remove the bag of pickling spices and pour the hot chutney into hot jars.
8 Seal down at once.

Quick pineapple relish

cooking time: 5 minutes

you will need:

1 tablespoon onion, chopped	1 tablespoon parsley, chopped
1 oz. butter	2 tablespoons mild mustard
4 tablespoons pineapple, shredded	

1 Gently fry onion in the butter until soft, but not brown.
2 Add pineapple, chopped parsley and mild mus-tard and mix well.
3 Use with any hot meat or poultry.

Mustard relish

cooking time: 30 minutes

you will need:

1 lb. onions	8 oz. sultanas,
3 lb. apples (weight	washed
after peeling)*	3 teaspoons dry
1½ pints vinegar	mustard
½ oz. mustard seed	1 lb. sugar
1 tablespoon salt	

*or 1 lb. tomatoes, 2 lb. apples.

1 Simmer the chopped onions and cored apples with half the vinegar, until tender, adding mustard seed tied up in muslin.
2 When soft put in remaining ingredients, blending the mustard with vinegar. Stir well until the sugar has dissolved, then boil steadily until thick, stirring from time to time.
3 Take out the bag of mustard seed. Pour into clean hot jars and seal.

Variation

Apple and red pepper relish – follow the recipe for mustard relish, but add one or two diced red peppers (capsicums) and use 2 lb. apples.

End of season relish

cooking time: 1½ hours

you will need:

2 lb. green tomatoes	½ medium cucumber,
(skinned)	peeled
¼ head white cabbage	3 rounded tablespoons
2 small capsicums	salt
(sweet red peppers)	5 oz. brown sugar
2 medium onions	1½ pints mild vinegar
8 oz. ripe tomatoes	2 level tablespoons
(skinned)	mild mustard
2 small green peppers	1 level teaspoon
2 medium stalks	paprika
celery	

1 Chop vegetables.
2 Place in pan in layers, sprinkling each layer with salt.
3 Stand overnight.
4 Drain and press out all liquid.
5 Add sugar, vinegar, mustard and paprika to vegetables.
6 Cook for about 1½ hours, stirring often.
7 Pour into clean hot jars and seal.

Tomato and horseradish relish

cooking time: 40–45 minutes

you will need:

¾ pint vinegar	1 large onion
1 dessertspoon	1 dessertspoon salt
pickling spice	½ teaspoon pepper –
4 lb. ripe tomatoes	preferably cayenne
(skinned)	or paprika
2 large cooking	horseradish*
apples	1 lb. sugar

*The amount of horseradish added depends entirely on personal taste, so add it gradually, tasting as you do so.

1 Boil the vinegar and pickling spices together for 10 minutes.
2 Cook the tomatoes, apples and onion until a thick pulp, stirring to begin with so that it does not burn.
3 Add vinegar, salt and pepper, remove spices.
4 Cook in an uncovered pan until it becomes thick. This will take a fair time.
5 Add 2–3 tablespoons grated horseradish and the sugar.
6 Boil again for about 10 minutes.
7 Put into boiling bottling jars.
8 Seal down and sterilise by standing these (with screw tops loosened) in a pan of boiling water and boiling rapidly for about 10 minutes.
9 Lift out jars carefully and tighten screw tops.

Salting beans

you will need:

3 lb. beans (runner or	1 lb. kitchen salt
French) – should be	(*not* free-running
young, fresh and	table salt)
tender	

Failures are often due to the use of too little salt, so it is better to adhere strictly to these quantities.

1 Wash, dry and remove strings.
2 French beans can be left whole, runner beans should be sliced.
3 Place a layer of salt in a glass or stoneware jar and on this a layer of beans.
4 Continue to fill the jar with alternate layers, pressing the beans well down and finishing with a layer of salt. If preferred, some salt can be used for the bottom and top layers and the rest

mixed with the beans before they are packed into the jars.

5 Cover and leave for a few days.
6 The beans will shrink and the jar should be filled up with more beans and salt, again having a layer of salt at the top. The salt does not remain dry, as it draws moisture from the beans and forms a strong brine – this should not be thrown away otherwise air pockets may be left between the layers of beans in which bacteria and moulds may develop.
7 When full, cork the jar securely.
8 If the beans become slimy and do not keep, insufficient salt has been added or the beans were not pressed down sufficiently when packed into jars.

To use the beans

9 Remove from the jar, wash thoroughly in several waters.
10 Leave to soak for 2 hours in warm water.
11 Cook in boiling water, without salt, until they are tender (25–35 minutes). Drain and serve in the same way as fresh runner beans.

Storing new potatoes

These can, of course, be stored by bottling, but you can also keep some to be used for Christmas Day by burying in sand in the garden in a sheltered place. They will not store for a very much longer period than this.

Storing nuts

The nuts should be gathered when they are mature, otherwise they will not store well.
Almonds – make certain that you are using the sweet almonds, because bitter almonds should not be eaten, although very small quantities can be added to cakes for flavouring.

1 Spread the nuts out in one flat layer to dry.
2 When dry put in containers, filling with a layer of nuts and a layer of salt and some kind of packing such as is used round grapes, if desired. If you cannot get this, use a layer of salt and a layer of nuts.
Chestnuts – store in boxes in a dry place.
Cob nuts – lay out in flat boxes in an airy space. Turn once or twice during storage.

Walnuts – remove the green husk before storing. Clean away any pieces of the husk, dry the nuts and store as almonds.

Nuts, to salt

Almonds, cashews, cob nuts, peanuts
Shell the nuts, then heat in butter or olive oil until they are a faint golden colour, and then toss in salt.
Store in airtight jars or tins. Almonds should be blanched and dried before salting.

Mint, preserving

Chop the washed mint finely and put a layer into a jar with an equal depth of sugar. Continue to fill the jar in the same way until full, finishing with a layer of sugar. Seal down.

Herbs, to dry

To dry herbs, wash them, after picking in hot weather. Dry well in a cloth, then lay them on baking trays padded with plenty of paper and a piece of muslin over the top. Dry very slowly in the airing cupboard or very low oven 200°F.– Gas Mark ¼ (with the door ajar), until brittle. Crumble and put into jars.
In hot weather they can be dried in the sun. Parsley is a better colour if dried for a few minutes in a hot oven.

Herbs, to freeze

Chopped fresh herbs may be preserved packed in ice cube containers in a home freezer. You can also store a number of bouquets garnis by placing sprigs of herbs between small squares of polythene in the freezer.

Chutneys made with a pressure cooker

A pressure cooker is ideal for softening fruits, etc., for chutney. You can do this in a very short time and make quite certain the skins really are soft before the sugar is added. Here are two recipes:

Green tomato chutney (2)

cooking time: 20 minutes

you will need:

3 lb. tomatoes	1 teaspoon salt
1 lb. sour apples	$\frac{1}{2}$ oz. root ginger
8 oz. onions	$\frac{1}{2}$ pint vinegar
8 oz. sultanas	8 oz. sugar

1 Remove skins of tomatoes, peel and core apples cut into very small pieces. Chop onions, tie ginger in muslin bag.
2 Put all ingredients except sugar into cooker (remove trivet) adding vinegar. Stir well, cover and bring to 10 lb. pressure. Pressure cook for 10 minutes.
3 Reduce pressure with cold water.
4 Stir in sugar and simmer in open cooker until chutney is of a thick smooth consistency. Remove ginger.
5 Put into warm jars, do not overfill, and seal.

Apple and marrow chutney

cooking time: 25 minutes

you will need:

2 lb. apples	2 cloves garlic
1 lb. marrow	$\frac{1}{2}$ tablespoon salt
1 lb. onions	$\frac{1}{2}$ pint vinegar
4 oz. crystallised ginger	allspice
$\frac{1}{4}$ teaspoon cayenne pepper	$1\frac{1}{2}$ lb. brown sugar

1 Peel, core and cut up the apples and marrow into small pieces and slice onions finely.
2 Put vinegar and all ingredients, except sugar, into cooker. Stir well, cover and bring to 10 lb. pressure. Pressure cook for 15 minutes.
3 Reduce pressure with cold water.
4 Stir in sugar and simmer without lid on cooker until chutney is of a thick consistency.
5 Put into warm jars and seal.

Ketchups or sauces

When tomatoes, etc. are cheap, it is well worthwhile making your own sauces or ketchups. Bottled correctly they keep for a long period and can be used as a 'short cut' to flavour any salad dressings, sauces, or as an accompaniment to meat, fish and other savoury dishes.

To fill and sterilise bottles of ketchup

1 You can use ordinary bottles providing you have corks that fit and the bottles are made of sufficiently strong glass to withstand heat.
2 Sterilise bottles by putting into pan of cold water and bringing up to boil – lift out on to WOODEN board – do not put on cold surface.
3 Pour *boiling* ketchup into the jar while hot – a funnel is the easiest way to do this.
4 When filled to within about $\frac{3}{4}$ inch of the top, stand bottles – lightly corked – in pan of boiling water with padding at base and boil steadily for 10 minutes. Take care bottles do not fall over.
5 Lift out and coat with wax – see below.

Note
If using bottling jars, proceed as for fruit pulp, see pages 73, 74.

Using wax on bottles of ketchup
If bottling ketchup in old lemonade or ketchup bottles, you MUST ensure that they are airtight.

1 To do this the filled sterilised bottles should be sealed down with clean corks as soon as they are lifted out from the steriliser.
2 Have hot melted candle or paraffin wax avail-

able and brush round the cork to make an air-tight seal.

3 If necessary repeat with second layer of wax, then cover with foil or paper.
4 If wished a tiny round of waxed paper can be put over the ketchup in the bottle – the moment it comes from being sterilised – then a teaspoon of melted candle or paraffin wax poured over the top. You can then cover with ordinary metal bottle tops.

Blackberry ketchup

cooking time: 45 minutes

you will need:

3 lb. blackberries	vinegar
½ pint water	salt
sugar	

1 Simmer the blackberries in the water until tender.
2 Rub through a sieve very firmly, leaving only the pips behind.
3 To each pint of purée, add 2 oz. sugar and ½ pint spiced vinegar (see page 56).
4 A little salt may also be added if you wish.
5 Simmer steadily until fairly thick.
6 Put into heated bottles and sterilise as for tomato and horseradish relish (see page 67). This ketchup is delicious with cold meat.

Damson ketchup

cooking time: 55 minutes

you will need:

3 lb. damsons	vinegar
1 pint water	salt
sugar	

1 Simmer the damsons in the water until tender.
2 Rub through a sieve very firmly, leaving only the stones behind.
3 To each pint purée allow 4 oz. sugar and ½ pint spiced vinegar (see page 56).
4 A little salt may also be added if you wish.
5 Simmer steadily until fairly thick.
6 Put into heated bottles and sterilise as for tomato and horseradish relish (see page 67). This ketchup is delicious with cold meat and corned beef hash.

Grape ketchup

cooking time: 50 minutes

Use recipe and method for blackberry ketchup, using grapes instead of blackberries. When adding sugar a better flavour is produced by using 4 oz. to each pint of purée.
This ketchup is very good with cold chicken.

Mushroom ketchup

cooking time: 2½ hours

you will need:

3 lb. mushrooms	1 level dessertspoon
3 oz. salt	onion, chopped
½ pint spiced vinegar	(optional)
(see page 56)	

1 Mince or break up mushrooms.
2 Sprinkle with salt and leave for 24–36 hours.
3 Add spiced vinegar to the mushrooms and liquor (with chopped onion if liked).
4 Simmer gently for 2½ hours.
5 Strain carefully through muslin while boiling.
6 Bottle in sterilised jars and sterilise them (see page 69).
7 Seal at once, coating corks with melted wax.

Spiced apple ketchup

cooking time: 1 hour

you will need:

4 lb. apples (after peeling and coring)	2 teaspoons salt
2 large onions, peeled	1 teaspoon curry powder
2 cloves garlic	½ teaspoon cayenne pepper
¾ pint brown vinegar	1 teaspoon turmeric
2 teaspoons pickling spices	8 oz. sugar

1 Chop the apples, onion and garlic, and cook with the pickling spices, vinegar and seasoning until the apples form a thick pulp.
2 Rub through a sieve, adding the sugar.
3 Boil rapidly until set.
4 Pour into hot bottles and sterilise (see page 69).

Tomato ketchup

cooking time: 1–1¼ hours

you will need:

¾ pint vinegar
1 dessertspoon pickling spice
4 lb. ripe tomatoes (skinned)
1 large onion, peeled
2 large cooking apples (peeled and cored)
6 oz. sugar
1 dessertspoon salt
¼ teaspoon paprika or cayenne

1 Boil the vinegar and pickling spices together for 10 minutes.
2 Then strain the vinegar.
3 Cook the sliced tomatoes, onion and apples until you have a thick pulp, stirring well to prevent mixture burning.
4 Rub through a sieve taking care not to leave any pulp behind, otherwise it will not thicken.
5 Put pulp into pan with vinegar, sugar, salt and pepper.
6 Cook steadily until thick.
7 Pour into sterilised bottles while boiling and sterilise for certain keeping (see page 69).
8 Seal down and if using corks paint at once with hot wax (see page 69).

Tomato and chilli ketchup

cooking time: 45 minutes

Use recipe and method for tomato ketchup, but add 2 chilli peppers, one chopped sweet red pepper and 1 clove of garlic.

18th century catchup

1 'Take mushrooms and wipe them very clean.
2 Put them in a crock and strew salt between every 2 or 3 handfuls.
3 Let them stand for 2 or 3 days.
4 Strain them off and boil up ye licker with cloves, mace, nutmeg and pepper, a pretty while.
5 When it is cold put it into a bottle and stop it very close.'
To make this today you might care to chop up the mushrooms coarsely and keep them in the liquor, after letting them stand. Adjust the spices to taste, but as mushrooms have a definite though delicate flavour, don't be too sparing.

Apple sauce

cooking time: 30 minutes, plus time for preserving

you will need:

1 lb. cooking apples (after peeling and coring)
¼ pint water
1 oz. margarine or butter
2 tablespoons sugar

1 Slice apples thinly.
2 Put into small saucepan adding about ¼ pint water, the margarine and the sugar.
3 Allow to simmer steadily until a smooth mixture.
4 Beat well with wooden spoon when apples are cooked, to give a good smooth appearance.

Spiced apple sauce

cooking time: 30 minutes, plus time for preserving

Use recipe and method for apple sauce, but add 1 teaspoon of mixed spice.

Bottling sweet sauces

You save a great deal of time if you prepare a large quantity of cranberry or apple sauce and preserve it for use at any period in the year. These are recommended recipes, and you must sterilise as for pulped fruit (see page 74).

Apple and cranberry sauce

cooking time: 30 minutes, plus time for preserving

Use recipe and method for apple sauce (see above but use 8 oz. apples and 8 oz. cranberries.

Cranberry sauce (1)

cooking time: 30 minutes, plus time for preserving

you will need:

2 tablespoons water	12 oz. cranberries
3 oz. sugar	1 tablespoon port or sherry

1 Heat water and sugar together.
2 Add the fruit and cook until tender.
3 Add port or sherry if wished.
4 Having prepared the sauce, pour boiling sauce into boiling hot jars and then proceed as for pulped fruit (see page 74).

Cranberry sauce (2)

cooking time: 30 minutes, plus time for preserving

you will need:

8–12 oz. cranberries	2–3 oz. sugar
¼ pint water	knob of butter

1 Simmer the cranberries in the water.
2 Rub through a sieve.
3 Add sugar to taste and the butter.

Mint sauce

cooking time: 5–15 minutes, plus time for preserving

you will need:

¼ pint vinegar	8 tablespoons mint
4 oz. sugar	

1 Boil the vinegar and sugar until sugar has dissolved.

2 Add the chopped mint.
3 Put into the smallest size preserving jars available.
4 Sterilise as for pulped fruit (see page 74).

Orange and raspberry sauce

cooking time: 30 minutes, plus time for preserving

Use recipe and method for apple sauce (see page 71), but use 8 oz. oranges and 8 oz. raspberries.

Redcurrant sauce

cooking time: 20 minutes, plus time for preserving

you will need:

1 lb. redcurrants	3–4 oz. sugar
¼ pint water	knob butter

1 Simmer the redcurrants with water and sugar until soft.
2 Rub through a sieve. Add butter.
3 Reheat with the pulp.
4 Proceed as for pulp fruit (see page 74).
This sauce is excellent with lamb or mutton.

Bottling fruit and vegetables

In order the have the best results, it is important to prepare the fruit carefully. The look of the bottles depends a great deal on the time you have given to preparing the fruit.

To prepare soft fruit

If this requires washing, place the soft fruit on a sieve and run cold water very gently over the fruit. Leave to drain.

To prepare hard fruit

If possible, try to wipe rather than wash the fruit as using too much water will tend to spoil the flavour.

Apples – peel, core and slice, and immediately drop into a bowl of salted water, i.e., 1 level tablespoonful kitchen salt to each quart of cold water. Let the apples stay there for 10 minutes, with a plate on top of them if desired, but this is not really necessary. This prevents the apples from becoming brown in colour.

Peaches – drop the peaches into boiling water and leave them there for $\frac{1}{2}$–1 minute. Remove and put into cold water, then skin them. Leave them in water until ready to pack the jars. This prevents their discoloration.

Pears – preparation of pears is similar to apples. If using hard cooking pears, simmer these until soft. If pears are ripe, then remove from the salt water and put for 1 minute only in boiling water or boiling syrup. Pears treated this way should remain absolutely white in colour.

Tomatoes – If desired to peel the tomatoes, then drop them into boiling water for $\frac{1}{2}$ minute, then put into cold water. The skins will immediately come off.

To sterilise fruit in the oven

The temperature of the oven is very important. With a gas oven use gas mark $\frac{1}{4}$, if the pressure is very good, or gas mark $\frac{1}{2}$. Set an electric oven 240°F.

Stand the jars on either an asbestos mat, several thicknesses of paper or cardboard, or a wooden board. Cover the tops of the jars with an old, clean tin lid.

While the jars are in the oven, put the glass lids and rubber bands on to boil, and boil these for 15 minutes. If using metal tops, just drop them for 1 minute into boiling water so that the lacquer is not damaged.

Here is given a table of the length of time to leave the fruit in the oven:

raspberries, loganberries (Do not pack these fruits too tightly, otherwise they form a solid block of fruit which is very difficult to sterilise.)	45 minutes
rhubarb, redcurrants, blackcurrants	50 minutes
plums, apples, blackberries, damsons, greengages and cherries	1 hour
whole peaches, whole apricots, halved peaches, halved apricots, pears	1$\frac{1}{4}$ hours
tomatoes	1$\frac{1}{2}$ hours

At the end of the given time, first check up that everything is handy, for the important thing about the oven method is speed when the jars are brought out. Have ready a kettle of boiling water or pan of boiling syrup. Remove jars one at a time from the oven. Place on to a wooden surface, pour over the boiling liquid, tapping the jar as you do so, until it completely overflows. If using a screw top jar, put on the rubber ring first, put on the top, hold on to this tightly, then either screw down, clip down or put on weight. Do not handle the jars any more than necessary for 24 hours. After this time, remove the screw band or clip and test to see if the lid is firm. It should be possible to lift the jars by the lid. When the jars have sealed there is no need to replace either the clip or screw band, and these can be used again.

Note
If the screw band is put on the jar, do this only loosely, and it is advisable to lightly grease the inside of the band. The oven method is suitable for all fruits, but not for pulping or tomatoes bottled in their own juice.

Tomatoes
These are improved in flavour if salt and sugar are added. To each 1 lb. tomatoes allow $\frac{1}{2}$ teaspoonful salt, $\frac{1}{4}$ teaspoonful sugar. Sprinkle into the jar before pouring on boiling water.

To bottle in a steriliser

Ideally one should have a deep steriliser so the jars can be completely covered or at least covered up to the neck. If you have not a proper steriliser, a bread-bin or very deep saucepan can be used.

Prepare the fruit. See instructions for doing this on pages 72–73. Pack the fruit into the jars, packing as tightly as possible. Fill the jars to the very top with COLD water or COLD sugar syrup. Put on the boiled rubber bands and the lids. If using the screw-band jars, turn these as tightly as possible, then unscrew for half a turn, so allowing for the expansion of the glass. If using the clip tops put the clip into position. When using the skin covering, put this and the special string first of all into hot water for a few minutes, then tie on the skin as tightly as possible. Put some sort of padding at the bottom of the steriliser; a wooden board, several thicknesses of paper or an old cloth will do.

Stand the jars on this, being careful they do not touch the sides of the pan, or each other. It is always preferable to completely cover the jars in the steriliser with cold water, but if this is not possible, fill the steriliser with cold water up to the necks of the jars, then either put on the lid or cover with a board or tea cloth, so keeping in the steam. Take 1½ hours to bring the water in the steriliser to simmering, i.e. 165–175°F. for all fruits except pears and tomatoes, in which case the water should be brought to 180–190°F. With all fruits (but the following exceptions) maintain these temperatures for 10 minutes: with pears, peaches and tomatoes maintain for 30 minutes. Before lifting out the jars bale out a little water so that it is easier and safer to lift them out. Stand the jars on a wooden surface and if using jars with screw bands, tighten these.

To test if jars have sealed

Leave the jars for 24 hours, then test by removing the clip or band and seeing if the lid is tight. If it is, and the jar can be lifted by the lid, then the jars have sealed.

Pulping fruit

Imperfect fruit can be used for pulping if the bruised or diseased part has been cut away, leaving the rest of the fruit perfect. You must not use over-ripe fruit for pulping since this could cause fermentation during storage.

Method of pulping

1 Stew the fruit, adding little or no water, and sugar to taste.
2 With tomatoes add ½ teaspoon sugar and ½ teaspoon salt to each lb. tomatoes.
3 The tomatoes can be skinned if wished.
4 Rub through a sieve if a very smooth purée is desired.
5 If sieving, bring to the boil once again.
6 While the fruits are cooking put tops of jars to boil for 10 minutes.

7 Drop in the rubber bands for a minute too.
8 Sterilise the jars also by heating well.
9 Put the boiling pulp into the very hot jars.
10 Put on the rubber bands and the tops.
11 Put on the screw bands or clips.
12 If using screw bands give ½ turn back to allow for the expansion of the top of the bottles.
13 Stand the jars in a steriliser or deep pan filled with BOILING water.
14 Boil for a good 5–8 minutes in the case of fruit pulp and a good 10 minutes for tomato pulp.
15 Lift out and tighten screw bands.
16 Test as all bottled fruit after 24 hours.

To make syrup for fruit bottling

Obviously the strength of syrup you use will depend very much on personal taste and also the fruit to be bottled. Peaches for example are best in a heavy, to very heavy, syrup. Plums on the other hand are best in a light to medium heavy syrup.

Light syrup	4 oz. sugar 1 pint water
Heavy syrup	8–10 oz. sugar 1 pint water
Very heavy syrup	12 oz.–1 lb. sugar 1 pint water

The lighter the syrup, the better the appearance of the fruit, so for show purposes, bottle fruit in a really light syrup. To make the syrup, boil the sugar and water together until the sugar has dissolved. If syrup is slightly cloudy, strain through very fine muslin.

Bottling fruit without liquid

A less usual method of bottling fruit is to add no liquid at all, so that when the jars are opened they contain only the fruit. Obviously the flavour of fruit bottled by this method is much the best, for it is not diluted by water or syrup. This method is particularly suitable for **tomatoes**. Other fruits that can be done this way are **raspberries, strawberries** (although these bottle less successfully than any fruit), **peaches** and **halved plums**. Do not try to use other fruits containing less juice.

To prepare the jars, wash them thoroughly and boil the rubber rings for 10 minutes. Skin tomatoes, then, if large, cut them into halves. Pack the tomatoes into the jars tightly, but being careful not to break them. Add $\frac{1}{2}$ teaspoon salt and $\frac{1}{2}$ teaspoon sugar to each lb. tomatoes. With other fruits simply pack the fruits into the jars with a sprinkling of sugar here and there in the jars. When the bottles are completely filled, put on the rubber rings. tops and clips or screw bands.

Note carefully

These jars may not now be sterilised in the oven, but **must** be sterilised in a deep pan, so loosen the screw bands and proceed exactly as given in the directions for bottling in a steriliser, giving exactly the same time and temperatures. When the jars are removed from the steriliser it will be found that the fruit has sunk down the jars a little; these cannot be filled up, so simply tighten the screw bands and test after 24 hours as usual.

Fruit bottling in a pressure cooker

If you have a pressure cooker, it is a very good idea to use it for bottling fruit. You must, however, be certain that you have a special 5 lb. weight to go on the cooker. Your pressure cooking book will probably give you instructions. However, here are some points that should be followed very carefully:

1 Prepare the fruit, see pages 72–73.
2 You cannot use other than proper bottling jars or the special clip tops that go over jam jars, in a pressure cooker.
3 Fill the jars as for the steriliser method (see page 73).
4 Pour 1 pint hot water into cooker, add 1 tablespoon vinegar to prevent cooker staining. Stand jars on inverted trivet. Do not allow jars to touch one another or side of cooker, Use paper between jars if they are likely to touch. If using ordinary jam jars, put cloth or layers of newspaper on the trivet to prevent breakage. Add extra $\frac{1}{4}$ pint water to allow for absorption by cloth or paper. When using electricity bring to pressure on low heat.

5 Fix cover, place on heat and bring to 5 lb. pressure in usual way. Process for time stated in table below.
6 Turn off heat and leave cooker on stove to reduce pressure at room temperature. When using an electric stove, move cooker gently away from heat. Do not reduce pressure with cold water as sudden cooling will crack jars. Open cooker, remove jars one at a time on to a cloth or wooden surface. Tighten screw bands and allow to cool. Test seal after 24 hours by inverting jars. If seal is not perfect re-process.

Timetable for bottling fruit (use 5 lb. pressure control)

Apples	3–4 minutes
Apricots	3–4 minutes
Blackberries	3–4 minutes
Blackcurrants	7 minutes
Cherries	7 minutes
Damsons	3–4 minutes
Gooseberries	3–4 minutes
Loganberries	3–4 minutes
Peaches	7 minutes
Pears	3–4 minutes
Plums	3–4 minutes
Raspberries	3–4 minutes
Redcurrants	7 minutes
Rhubarb	3–4 minutes
Tomatoes	7 minutes

Bottling fruit for show purposes

1 Check before leaving the jars that the seal is still airtight because carrying sometimes breaks this seal and your jams will be automatically disqualified.
2 Make certain that the jars are well polished on

the outside. This helps to show off the fruit inside to advantage.

3 When bottling fruit use a fairly light syrup for this gives a better colour and prevents any possibility of the fruit rising in the jar.

4 See that the jars are labelled very carefully.

5 Pack very much more carefully and in a more original manner than you would for home bottling.

Suggested ways of packing fruit in bottles

Apples
These look very good cut in rings rather than slices and the rings packed round the outside with a blackberry in the centre of each, where the core has been removed.

Whole apples
Peeled and cored these look most interesting. If slicing apples make sure the slices are all turned to face the same way.

Apricots
Turn halved apricots with their cut side towards the jar and put a cracked kernel in the centre of each.

Blackberries
Fill jars with alternate layers of blackberries and sliced apples.

Cherries
These form a very attractive jar when mixed with halved apricots.

Gooseberries
Take care to select gooseberries that are the same size and degree of ripeness.

Grapes
Pack alternate black and white grapes in a jar.

Grapefruit
Arrange the sections to form a very definite design round the sides of the jar.

Greengages
Be very careful to choose fruit that is of even size and not over-ripe.

Oranges
Whole oranges are most effective bottled and these can be bottled in water rather than syrup.

Pears
Take great care with the colour of pears. It is quite a good idea, for show purposes, to put a little lemon juice into the syrup to make certain that the fruit keeps particularly white.

Small pears
These look very effective if peeled, cored and packed whole. This means turning some one way and some the other.

Peaches
The yellow cling peaches are the best for bottling and look wonderful when halved.

Pineapple
This can be bottled as whole rings, or halved rings with cherries to give contrasting colour.

Raspberries
These are most effective if a white or redcurrant is put into the centre of each and this turned towards the outside of the jar.

Rhubarb
The right way to pack rhubarb for show purposes is to make sure every piece is exactly the same length.

Strawberries
The best way to keep the colour of strawberries is to let them stand in cold syrup overnight, take out of the syrup, pack in the jars, add the syrup and use the steriliser method.

Fruit salad
Another most attractive pack of fruit for competition is a mixed fruit salad but do remember to sterilise this for the time required by the fruit wanting the longest period.

Bottling strawberries

Strawberries can be bottled by any of the methods given, but they tend to lose their flavour very easily. The way that seems to retain it more than any other is to put the strawberries into a boiling syrup with a little lemon juice to flavour, if wished. Allow to cool in syrup, then bottle by steriliser method.

Bottling fruit in brandy

1 All fruit can be bottled in brandy, but since it is a very expensive method, only the very luxurious fruits are generally used.
2 Use fruits suggested.
3 Prepare the fruit (see page 72).
4 Where the fruit has a firm skin, e.g. damsons, prick once or twice with a needle so that the brandy syrup can penetrate the fruit.
5 Pack the fruit into jars.
6 Make a fairly heavy syrup (see page 74).
7 To each pint of **cold** syrup, allow ¼ pint brandy.
8 Cover the fruit with the brandy flavoured syrup.
9 Proceed using the steriliser method or you can use the oven method for suitable fruits (see page 73).

Peaches in brandy	– see previous method.
Pears in brandy	– see previous method.
Dessert cherries in brandy	– see previous method.
Raspberries in brandy	– see previous method.
Damsons in brandy	– see previous method.

Bottling vegetables

Remember it is *unsafe* to bottle vegetables other than in a pressure cooker. Always follow the special instructions for your own make of pressure cooker. Below are the main points to remember.

1 Wash thoroughly to free vegetables from all traces of soil. Pre-cook or blanch by immersing in boiling water for the time stated in table below, then dropping into cold water. Drain well and pack into clean jars to within 1 inch of top. Do not pack too tightly.

TIMETABLE FOR BOTTLING VEGETABLES

(Use 10 lb. Pressure Control)

	Vegetables	Preparation	Minutes to blanch in boiling water	Minutes to process at 10 lb. pressure
1	Asparagus	Wash, trim off scales, cut in even lengths, tie in bundles, pack upright	2–3 minutes	40 minutes
2	Beans, Broad	Pod, choose very young beans	5 minutes	55 minutes
3	Beans, Runner	Wash, string and slice	5 minutes	40 minutes
4	Beetroot	Cut off top. Blanch before slicing or dicing	15–20 minutes	40 minutes
5	Carrots	Wash, scrape, slice or dice. Young new, leave whole	10 minutes	45 minutes
6	Celery	Wash, cut in even lengths	6 minutes	40 minutes
7	Corn	Strip from cob	2–3 minutes	50 minutes
8	Peas	Wash, shell and grade	2–3 minutes	50 minutes
9	Potatoes, New	Wash, scrape carefully or peel thinly	5 minutes	50 minutes

2 Still leaving 1 inch at top, cover vegetables with a hot brine solution, made by dissolving 2–3 oz. salt to 8 pints water, boiled before using. Work out air bubbles by quickly twisting the jar from side to side. Adjust rings and lids.

3 Process jars of hot food immediately. Pour 1 pint hot water into cooker, add 1 tablespoon vinegar. Stand jars on inverted trivet. Do not allow jars to touch each other on the sides of the cooker. Use paper between jars if necessary. Fix cover, place on LOW heat. Do not put on pressure control; allow air to be expelled through centre vent for 5 minutes. Put on 10 lb. pressure control valve, still at low heat, bring to pressure. Process for the times stated before. See that there is always a steady flow of steam from the pressure control as pressure must not drop below 10 lb.

4 As point 6 in fruit bottling (see page 75).

5 The loss of liquid does not interfere with the keeping quality of the food. Jars should never be opened, after processing, to replace liquid that has boiled away. When opening a jar of bottled vegetables do not taste the cold food. If the contents of the jar do not smell right and the food is soft and mushy, discard it at once. As a safeguard, heat bottled vegetables at boiling temperature for 10–15 minutes before tasting or using.

Bottling vegetables for show purposes

The same points apply here as were given under bottling fruit (see page 75), but the following points will help you to produce perfect jars of vegetables.

1 Choose vegetables of all the same size.

2 Potatoes should be put in a little salt water with lemon juice added to make certain they keep very white.

3 A few drops of green colouring can be added to the brine for peas and beans, but some judges do not approve of this.

To make certain screw top jars are easy to remove

When you have tested the jars and you are satisfied they have sealed properly, you should then grease or oil inside the metal bands. Replace the bands, but do not attempt to screw down very tightly. If using clip tops to the jars, grease the under-side of these very lightly and just lay to one side of the tops so they do not fit too tightly.

Home freezing

Never attempt to freeze foods (except ice cream and ice and frozen desserts) in the ordinary freezing compartment of a domestic refrigerator. A home freezer, which has a much lower temperature, must be used.

General rules for home freezing

1. Food

Only first-quality foods should be preserved by this method. Fruits and vegetables should be frozen directly they are picked. Meat and poultry should hang for the correct minimum length of time before freezing.

When this is not possible, all foods should be put in a cool place or household refrigerator for not longer than 12–24 hours before being prepared for the home freezer.

2. Packaging

Moisture-vapour-proof packaging materials are essential for freezing and storing produce.

Food will lose moisture by evaporation unless well packed and sealed, because of the low humidity inside the freezer. The food will become dry, the texture and colour deteriorate and the flavour will disappear. Badly packaged strong-smelling food may spoil other produce stored in the same freezer.

Therefore, choose packaging material with care and leave as little air as possible inside the containers before sealing.

3. Equipment

Quality of frozen food depends on speed, i.e. speed in preparation and quick drop in temperature when in the freezer.

4. For freezing set freezer at –20°F. to –30°F. For storing set freezer at 0°F.

To freeze small quantities quickly

(a) This method, by restricting the size of the ice crystals formed from the natural juices in food, minimises any change in its cell structure.

(b) With the shorter freezing time, there is less time for the separation of water in the form of ice, so less mineral salts are lost through seepage as the foods defrost.

(c) In this rapid freezing process there is quick cooling of the food to temperatures at which bacteria, moulds and yeast cannot grow. Therefore, foods are protected from the possibility of deterioration during freezing.

N.B. Do not overload the freezer, i.e. for the best results do not freeze too much food at one time.

To store

The lower the temperature, the longer the food can be kept stored and remain nearly perfect in flavour, colour and food value.

Loss of nutrients in frozen food

–40°F.	none
–10°F.	negligible
0°F.	very slow
10°F. or higher	much accelerated and in a comparatively short time the frozen food becomes rancid and unpleasant flavours set in.

Freezing already cooked food

A great variety of cooked foods can be frozen e.g.:

Bread
This enables you to cook a large batch of loaves and freeze them until required.

Cooked meats, fish and savoury dishes
Allow food to become quite cold, then freeze immediately while they are still very fresh. Where the wrapping may be placed on to the cold, cooked food, wrap before freezing. If, however, the wrapping would spoil the appearance of the cooked food, freeze then wrap. Once frozen you can lift puddings out of their basins to save space; or line the basin with foil before cooking, lift out the foil and food after freezing.

Cakes
Sponges – rich layer cakes – all freeze very well. Allow to cool and freeze while still fresh. Wrap as meat, etc.
Use your frozen food cabinet to save valuable time when planning menus.

Home freezing of raw foods
Meat

1 Choose only the best quality young tender meat for home freezing. Cut the meat into portions suitable for the purpose. It is wise to ask the butcher to do this.

2 Wrap larger pieces of meat, or portions, or joints, in moisture-vapour-proof covers, e.g. cellophane. Expel the air, turn in the edges and seal down with tape or by heat.

3 Smaller cuts, e.g. chops or steaks, are separated by two pieces of grease-proof paper in order that the required number may be removed without defrosting the rest.

4 Place in container, e.g. plastic bag and squeeze to expel the air. Seal by heat, sealing tape or bag fasteners. Turn in the sharp ends to avoid piercing packages.

5 After sealing over-wrap with mutton cloth or similar wrapping to protect from damage while in the freezer. Mark each package with date and weight of meat.

Poultry

1 Before freezing prepare poultry for cooking –

wrap sharp ends of the bird to protect the container. Wash and wrap giblets separately in moisture-vapour-proof materials.

2 Place the bird in suitable container, e.g. plastic bag. Place the giblets with it in container, expel the air and seal. Label with weight of bird and date frozen.

3 Pack carefully jointed poultry in a special tray. Separate the portions – if not to be used all at once – by two pieces of grease-proof paper.

4 Wrap poultry and tray in moisture-vapour-proof cellophane. Expel the air, turn in the edges, seal. Record weight and date on package with a chinagraph pencil.

Vegetables

1 Blanch all vegetables by immersing in boiling water. Bring to boil again. Time boiling according to the size of vegetables, e.g. boil for 1 minute. Cool, pack and seal.

2 Blanched and cooled vegetables may be packed in various types of containers, e.g. polythene bags. All vegetables **must** be blanched before packing and freezing.

3 After blanching in boiling water, the vegetables should be drained and cooled. Place in bag, expel air and seal.

Fruit

1 Place clean, freshly picked fruit in a polythene bag. Cover with cooled syrup. Expel air and seal bag by heating.

2 The syrup should be poured to within half-an-inch of lid to allow for expansion during freezing. Alternatively, sugar can be sprinkled over the fruit.

Sealing containers for home freezing

Whether you are freezing raw or cooked foods, the containers must be firmly sealed. You can buy small strips of plastic for the tops of bags, or use adhesive tape.

Fruit syrups, glacé and crystallised fruits

All fruit syrups will keep well – they tend to have a better flavour as well as a thicker texture if sugar is added – but they can be preserved without if it should be necessary for medical reasons.

1 Put the fruit into the top of a double saucepan or basin over hot water, adding the water if required. Press down the fruit to squash it well and cook for about 1 hour until you are sure all the juice is extracted. Press down during cooking.

2 Strain through a jelly bag, or through several thicknesses of muslin over a fine sieve.

3 Measure the juice and add sugar, heat together until the sugar is dissolved, stirring well during this time. **Do not continue boiling** when sugar has dissolved.

4 Pour the hot syrup into hot bottling jars or use cordial bottles with well fitting screw topped lids, which should have been boiled before using.

5 Allow syrup to cool in the bottles, which should not be quite filled.

6 Stand them in a steriliser or deep pan with a rack at the bottom, or several thicknesses of cloth or paper.

7 Loosen screw bands $\frac{1}{4}$ turn, then take 1 hour to bring water to simmering (170°F). Retain for 30 minutes for large jars or bottles, or 20 minutes for smaller ones.

8 Lift out carefully, stand on a wooden surface and tighten screw bands.

9 Tie adhesive tape around the corks or caps of cordial bottles.

10 Dilute with water to serve.

To use fruit syrups

Fruit syrups can be used diluted with soda water in cold drinks, with milk for milk shakes, or used as a sauce poured over ice cream, or cold desserts of many kinds.

Variations of fruit syrup

Blackberry syrup

cooking time: 1 hour, plus sterilising time

you will need:

¼ pint water to each
  lb. fruit

8–12 oz. sugar to each
  pint of juice

Use method for fruit syrups (see page 80).

Blackcurrant syrup

cooking time: 1 hour, plus sterilising time

Allow ¼ pint water
  to each lb. black-
  currants

To each pint of juice
  allow 8–12 oz. sugar

Use method for fruit syrups (see page 80).

Cherry syrup

cooking time: 1 hour, plus sterilising time

you will need:

¼ pint water to each
  lb. very ripe juicy
  black cherries

8–12 oz. sugar to each
  pint of juice

Use method for fruit syrups (see page 80).

Damson syrup

cooking time: 1 hour, plus sterilising time

you will need:

⅜ pint water to
  each lb. fruit

12 oz. sugar to each
  pint of juice

Use method for fruit syrups (see page 80).

Elderberry syrup

cooking time: 1 hour, plus sterilising time

you will need:

1 lb. elderberries
¼ pint water

8 oz. sugar to each
  pint juice

Use method for fruit syrups (see page 80).

Lemonade syrup

cooking time: 5 minutes, plus sterilising time

you will need:

8 lemons
½ pint water

8–12 oz. sugar to
  each pint of juice

1 Peel the lemons very thinly to remove rind only.
2 Put peel into a pan with the water.
3 Simmer for 5 minutes.
4 Strain and add to the lemon juice.
5 Measure and add the sugar.
6 Proceed as step 3 in fruit syrups (see page 80).

Loganberry syrup

cooking time: 1 hour, plus sterilising time

you will need:

1 lb. loganberries
2 tablespoons water

8–12 oz. sugar to each
  pint of juice

Use method as for fruit syrups (see page 80).

Orangeade syrup

cooking time: 5 minutes, plus sterilising time

you will need:

10 oranges
½ pint water

8–12 oz. sugar to each
  pint of juice

Use method for lemonade syrup.

Raspberry syrup

cooking time: just under 1 hour, plus sterilising time

you will need:

8–12 oz. sugar to
  each pint of
  raspberry juice

no water required

Use method for fruit syrups (see page 80).

Redcurrant syrup

cooking time: 1 hour, plus sterilising time

you will need:

¼ pint water to each
  lb. of fruit

8–12 oz. sugar to each
  pint of juice

Use method as for fruit syrups (see page 80).

Rhubarb syrup

cooking time: 1 hour, plus sterilising time

you will need:

¼ pint water to each lb. fruit

12 oz. sugar to each pint of juice

Use method for fruit syrups (see page 80).

Rose hip syrup

cooking time: 5 minutes, plus sterilising time

you will need:

1 lb. rosehips
3 pints water

8–12 oz. sugar to each pint juice

To preserve the maximum amount of vitamin C, this is the method to use:

1 Grate or chop the hips quickly and use immediately after grating.
2 Put into the water when boiling.
3 Simmer for 5 minutes only.
4 Stand for 15 minutes.
5 Strain and measure.
6 Add the sugar and proceed from step 3 in fruit syrups (see page 80).

Strawberry syrup

cooking time: just under 1 hour, plus sterilising time

you will need:

8–12 oz. sugar per pint of juice

no water required

Use method for fruit syrups (see page 80).

Fruit juices

These are made and bottled in exactly the same way as the fruit syrups (see recipes), but are meant to be served undiluted, so only 2–4 oz. sugar is used to each pint of juice.
Fruit juice is delightfully refreshing and makes an ideal drink when served with ice in summer.

Glacé fruits

Fresh fruits: Oranges, Pears, Grapes, Cherries.
Canned fruit: Mandarins, Pineapple pieces, Pears, Lychees.

Fresh fruits

Sections of oranges and halved small pears and grapes are suitable.

1 Choose firm fruits, wash and divide into neat segments.
2 Cook gently in water until just tender. Grapes need no cooking – they should be put into the dish and the syrup poured over.
3 For each lb. of fruit allow ½ pint of syrup. Make this up by using ½ pint of the water in which the fruits were cooked, and 6 oz. sugar.
4 Put the fruit into a fairly shallow dish and pour the syrup over while warm. Leave for 24 hours well covered: put a plate on top of the dish.
5 Pour off the syrup and re-boil, adding another 2 oz. sugar. Pour over fruit again and leave for another 24 hours.
6 *Repeat* this another 3 times – each time adding an extra 2 oz. sugar.
7 Drain off the fruit, return the syrup to the pan, this time adding 3 oz. sugar to the original ½ pint syrup. When boiling, add the fruit and boil for 3 minutes. Return to the dish and leave for 24 hours.
8 Repeat step No. 7. The syrup should then take on the consistency of thick honey. If thin, repeat once again.
9 Drain off the syrup and place the fruit on a wire cake rack to dry – leave a plate underneath to catch the drips.

Canned fruits

1 Drain the fruit from the syrup.
2 Measure the syrup, and to each ½ pint add 2 oz. sugar. Boil together, pour over fruit and leave for 24 hours. Continue as for fresh fruit from step No. 4 to end.

Note
The syrup can be coloured if desired.

Crystallised fruits

Fresh fruit: Oranges, Pears, Grapes, Cherries.
Canned fruits: Mandarins, Pineapple pieces, Pears, Lychees
Follow instructions for *Glacé fruits*, steps 1 to 9, then

10 Put the fruit into the oven (225°F. – Gas Mark ¼) with the door slightly ajar. Leave until crisp. (An alternative is to roll and coat in granulated sugar.)

Crystallised angelica

1 Choose stalks that are young, firm and tender.
2 Cut off the root ends and leaves, then place the stalks in a basin and pour over a boiling brine (make this with ¼ oz. kitchen salt to 4 pints water).
3 Allow to soak for 10 minutes then rinse in cold water.
4 Place in a saucepan of fresh boiling water. Boil for 5 minutes if very tender – a little longer if somewhat older.
5 Drain well, then scrape off outer skin.
6 Continue in exactly the same way as from step 3, Crystallised fruits. Store in dry jars – the colour will keep better if kept in a dark place.

Crystallised flowers

Flowers: Roses, Violets, Primroses, Polyanthus.
Blossoms: Plum, Cherry, Apple, Pear, Heather.

Note
Non-edible flowers are those which come from bulbs – in many cases these are poisonous.

you will need:

1 oz. gum arabic rosewater (triple strength)	flowers castor sugar

1 Cover the gum arabic with the rosewater and leave for 24 hours to melt.
2 When properly melted, paint each petal of the flowers all over on both sides, using a fine paint brush, then hold each flower by the stem and sprinkle with castor sugar all over it.

Candied peel

Candied orange peel

you will need:

peel of 8 sweet oranges ½ oz. bicarbonate of soda	water 1½ lb. granulated sugar

1 Well wash the oranges.
2 Remove the skin in quarters and discard as much pith as possible.
3 Dissolve the bicarbonate of soda in 2 quarts boiling water and soak the peel for 20–30 minutes.
4 Strain and simmer gently in fresh water until tender.
5 Take out peel and immerse in a hot syrup made from 1 lb. sugar dissolved in 1 pint water brought to boiling point. Leave to soak for 2 days, covering with a plate.
6 Drain off syrup and add 8 oz. sugar. Bring to the boil and simmer peel until clear. Put on a rack to drain and dry (this can be done in a cool oven).
7 The next day, boil up the remaining syrup and dip pieces of peel in this, then dry again and store in covered jars.

Variations
Candied lemon peel, Candied grapefruit peel – follow the same procedure as for Candied orange peel.

Flavoured vinegars

Flavouring vinegar by the use of herbs or fruit provides an excellent variety, so that when you make salad dressings you can give a new flavour. Some people like to drink fruit flavoured vinegars and many people consider that in winter they are very beneficial.

Fruit vinegar

cooking time: 10 minutes

1 Allow 1 pint vinegar to each lb. of soft fruit, unless otherwise stated.
2 Add the vinegar to the fruit.
3 Leave for 3–5 days – stirring occasionally.
4 Strain off liquid.
5 Add 8 oz.–1 lb. sugar to each pint, depending on personal taste.
6 Boil for 10 minutes and bottle.
7 Use these fruit vinegars as the basis of dressings with salads or many people like a little mixed with sugar and hot water as a winter drink.

Blackcurrant vinegar

Use recipe and method for fruit vinegar, but use ordinary malt or white malt vinegar. Rather small blackcurrants can be used for this.

Elderberry vinegar

cooking time: 10 minutes

1 Allow 1 pint white vinegar to each 12 oz. fruit.
2 Add the vinegar to the fruit and proceed as for fruit vinegar (see above) adding 12 oz. sugar to each pint of vinegar.

Horseradish vinegar

you will need:

horseradish   white vinegar

1 Scrape and shred the horseradish with a coarse grater.
2 Pack into jars, half filling each jar.
3 Pour over cold vinegar.
4 Store for 6 weeks, shaking the bottles daily if possible.
5 Strain the vinegar through very fine muslin.
   This is excellent for salad dressings to serve with cold beef.

Mint vinegar

Use recipe and method for thyme vinegar, but use whole mint leaves. This is ideal for mint flavoured dressings.

Raspberry vinegar

Use recipe and method for fruit vinegar – preferably use ripe dry fruit – but this is a good way to use up any fruit that might be 'squashed' at the bottom of the basket. White malt vinegar gives a better colour.

Redcurrant vinegar

Use recipe and method for fruit vinegar, but use ordinary malt or white malt vinegar. The rather small redcurrants can be used for this.

Sage vinegar

you will need:

sage leaves   malt or white vinegar

1 Bruise the sage leaves by crushing with a rolling pin to extract flavour.
2 Pack them into jars, half filling each jar.
3 Pour over cold vinegar.
4 Store for 6 weeks, shaking the bottles daily if possible.
5 Strain the vinegar through very fine muslin. Ideal for mayonnaise or dressing to serve with cold pork or duck.

Tarragon vinegar

you will need:

tarragon leaves   malt or white vinegar

1 Bruise the tarragon leaves by crushing with a rolling pin, to extract flavour.
2 Pack them into jars, half filling each jar.

3 Pour over cold vinegar.
4 Store for 6 weeks, shaking the bottles daily if possible.
5 Strain the vinegar through very fine muslin. Use for fish salads and in béarnaise sauce or hollandaise sauce.

Thyme vinegar

you will need:

thyme – lemon   malt or white vinegar
flavoured thyme
particularly good

1 Bruise the thyme leaves by crushing with a rolling pin to extract flavour.
2 Pack them into jars, half filling each jar.
3 Pour over cold vinegar.
4 Store for 6 weeks, shaking the bottles daily if possible.
5 Strain the vinegar through very fine muslin. Ideal for mayonnaise or dressing to serve with cold chicken or turkey.

Savoury butters

Flavoured butters

Anchovy – cream butter and add a few drops anchovy essence.

Chutney – cream butter and add a spoonful or two of chutney.

Curry – cream butter and add $\frac{1}{2}$ teaspoon curry powder to 2 oz. butter.

Herbs – cream butter and blend in chopped thyme, marjoram, mint, sage or parsley, etc.

Lemon – add grated lemon rind and a little lemon juice to creamed butter.

Mustard – blend in made-mustard and chopped watercress.

Watercress – chop watercress and blend in.

Barbecue – add a few drops of Worcestershire sauce.

Seasoned butter

1 Rub bowl with a clove of garlic.
2 Cream 4 oz. butter until fluffy.
3 Beat into butter 1 tablespoon mild mustard, 1 tablespoon finely chopped parsley, 1 teaspoon finely chopped onion or chives.

Devilled mustard butter

Blend 4 oz. butter or margarine with $\frac{1}{2}$ tablespoon made-mustard, $\frac{1}{2}$ teaspoon curry powder, 1 tablespoon lemon juice and $\frac{1}{4}$ teaspoon finely grated lemon rind. (This is excellent with fish sandwiches, hot or cold.)

Ham butter

Mince 2 oz. lean ham or bacon and mix into 2 oz. butter or margarine to form a smooth paste.

Index